The Pharmaceutical Industry

Trade Related Issues

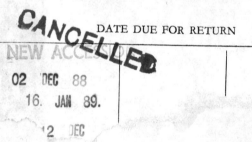
ORGANISATION FOR ECONOMIC CO-OPERATION AND DEVELOPMENT

Pursuant to article 1 of the Convention signed in Paris on 14th December, 1960, and which came into force on 30th September, 1961, the Organisation for Economic Co-operation and Development (OECD) shall promote policies designed:

- to achieve the highest sustainable economic growth and employment and a rising standard of living in Member countries, while maintaining financial stability, and thus to contribute to the development of the world economy;
- to contribute to sound economic expansion in Member as well as non-member countries in the process of economic development; and
- to contribute to the expansion of world trade on a multilateral, non-discriminatory basis in accordance with international obligations.

The Signatories of the Convention on the OECD are Austria, Belgium, Canada, Denmark, France, the Federal Republic of Germany, Greece, Iceland, Ireland, Italy, Luxembourg, the Netherlands, Norway, Portugal, Spain, Sweden, Switzerland, Turkey, the United Kingdom and the United States. The following countries acceded subsequently to this Convention (the dates are those on which the instruments of accession were deposited): Japan (28th April, 1964), Finland (28th January, 1969), Australia (7th June, 1971) and New Zealand (29th May, 1973).

The Socialist Federal Republic of Yugoslavia takes part in certain work of the OECD (agreement of 28th October, 1961).

Publié en français sous le titre:

L'INDUSTRIE PHARMACEUTIQUE
Questions liées aux échanges

This study has been undertaken within the general framework of the OECD's joint work on issues in trade in high technology products of the Industry Committee and the Committee for Scientific and Technological Policy. It is one of four case studies of high technology industries undertaken in this context, the others concerning the machine tool, semiconductor and space products' industries. The study was prepared by the OECD Secretariat with the assistance of Dr. M.L. Burstall, University of Surrey (United Kingdom), and Mme C. Michon-Savarit, consultant to OECD. The Committee for Scientific and Technological Policy and the Industry Committee recommended derestriction of this study in August 1984. The study is published under the responsibility of the Secretary-General of the OECD.

Also available

PETROCHEMICAL INDUSTRY – ENERGY ASPECTS OF STRUCTURAL CHANGE (February 1985)
(58 85 01 1) ISBN 92-64-12683-X   162 pages   £9.50   US$19.00   F95.00

THE SEMICONDUCTOR INDUSTRY: TRADE RELATED ISSUES (February 1985)
(93 85 01 1) ISBN 92-64-12687-2   146 pages   £9.50   US$19.00   F95.00

LONG TERM OUTLOOK FOR THE WORLD AUTOMOBILE INDUSTRY (March 1984)
(70 83 04 1) ISBN 92-64-12523-X   118 pages   £7.60   US$15.00   F76.00

ALUMINIUM INDUSTRY. Energy Aspects of Structural Change (December 1983)
(70 83 03 1) ISBN 92-64-12519-1   136 pages   £6.60   US$13.00   F66.00

INDUSTRIAL ROBOTS. Their Role in Manufacturing Industry (November 1983)
(70 83 02 1) ISBN 92-64-12486-1   94 pages   £4.90   US$9.75   F49.00

INNOVATION IN SMALL AND MEDIUM FIRMS. Background Reports (February 1982)
(92 82 01 1) ISBN 92-64-12277-X   300 pages   £6.80   US$15.00   F68.00

INNOVATION POLICY. Trends and Perspectives for the 1980s (January 1982)
(92 81 06 1) ISBN 92-64-12263-X   200 pages   £4.80   US$10.75   F48.00

TECHNICAL CHANGE AND ECONOMIC POLICY. Science and Technology in the New Economic and Social Context (August 1980)
(92 80 01 1) ISBN 92-64-12102-1   118 pages   £5.60   US$12.50   F50.00

Prices charged at the OECD Publications Office.

*THE OECD CATALOGUE OF PUBLICATIONS and supplements will be sent free of charge
on request addressed either to OECD Publications Office,
2, rue André-Pascal, 75775 PARIS CEDEX 16, or to the OECD Sales Agent in your country.*

TABLE OF CONTENTS

Chapter I

INTRODUCTION

The pharmaceutical industry possesses a number of features which are common to other technology-intensive industries, in particular an above-average growth rate which depends to a large extent on continued product innovation based on high R&D expenditures. It also shows some distinctive characteristics which make it unique in this class. In the context of an examination of trade related issues, two of these characteristics seem to be of particular relevance.

First, the industry has been the object of considerable government regulation and supervision for many years. All national administrations control the admission of new drugs to domestic markets for reasons of safety; most of them regulate the prices at which they are sold; and many supervise aspects of manufacture and marketing to a greater or lesser degree.

Second, the industry is one in which foreign direct investment has played an important part for several decades. Almost all companies of any significance have adopted a transnational form of organisation. They not only maintain sales forces in many countries, but manufacture drugs in a number of them and carry out research in a few of them. Firms of this type dominate the world pharmaceutical industry: the top 25 [see Table A8 in Annex] account for nearly one-half of total output, and the top 50 for about two-thirds.

This strategy has been followed for many years and is now seen as a natural feature of the industry. It is made feasible by a number of the technical characteristics of manufacturing and marketing in pharmaceuticals and fostered by two sets of factors: the nature of competition between very large firms, and the forms taken by government regulation and supervision which have often made the multinational form of organisation a necessity (1).

The role played by foreign direct investment means that despite the low volume and high unit value of its products and their low transport costs, the pharmaceutical industry sends a surprisingly small proportion of its output across national frontiers. In 1980, world sales were about $85 000 million in value, of which only $8 000 million -- less than 10 per cent -- entered international trade in the form of finished drugs, and a further $6 000 million in the form of intermediates (2). Local production by affiliates of multinational enterprises was over twice the size of direct imports in the same year [see Table 1].

7

In previous studies the effects of government regulation on the growth of the industry have been discussed mainly in relation to innovation. Less attention has been paid up to now to the effects of government action on the pattern of trade and the development of the multinational system. The effects on innovation on the one hand and on trade and investment on the other are, however, fairly closely related, notably in that part of pharmaceutical production which may properly be described as having a genuine "high-technology" character.

The industry is in fact composed of several segments with sharply differing features. Novel drugs, based on extensive research, developed by elaborate procedures, and protected by patent, clearly fall in the high-technology category. The firms which produce them represent the driving force of the industry as it is understood today. At the same time, in all countries a substantial proportion of production and sales is made up of out-of-patent generic and "over-the-counter" drugs. Since this report is primarily concerned with trade issues in the high technology part of the industry, it emphasises the production and trade of patented drugs, the process of innovation which underlies them, and the factors which may affect either.

As is shown later in this report, the rate at which new drugs are introduced fell in the early 60s, but has been stable since. Government regulation regarding the safety of products is one factor among several which have affected the cost of R&D and innovation and driven R&D thresholds constantly higher. A notable feature of the industry's development of the past twenty years has been the increasing concentration of innovation among large firms due, notably, to increasing difficulties of small firms to meet the cost of innovation. This has, to a large extent, been an unwanted result of some aspects of government action. While the evidence is inconclusive regarding the effect of government action on the rate of innovation, the data suggests that it may have undoubtedly hastened the process of concentration in the high technology segment of the industry.

Two significant trade related issues have nonetheless been identified at a general level of analysis:

i) The first relates to the persisting differences which exist from country to country with regard to the regulatory procedures ruling the approval of new drugs and their subsequent admission on the market. The report notes the extreme slowness with which international harmonisation of such procedures has progressed, even in cases where -- as in the EEC -- the ground work for such harmonisation has been accomplished;

ii) The second concerns the effect on trade of the controls exercised by governments over the price of drugs. In many Member countries the current economic crisis has considerably increased the intensity of government action on the price of drugs with the aim of reducing national health expenditures. Differences in the price of identical products from country to country have increased over the last years and led to a novel situation of "parallel imports", which represent a notable departure from healthy trade flows.

8

Chapter II

THE NATURE OF THE INDUSTRY AND DOMINANT PATTERNS OF OPERATION

Pharmaceuticals are a central element in health care. For many conditions they are the only, for others the cheapest and most effective, form of treatment. In most developed countries expenditure on drugs, at retail prices, amounts to between 10 and 20 per cent of health care spending, and 0.5-1.25 per cent of national income. In the Third World pharmaceuticals are relatively even more important, and sometimes account for as much as one quarter or one third of medical care.

Almost all countries, including the newly industrialised and many developing countries, have a drug industry of some kind or other, which caters for a part of the nation's needs. This is generally the result of deliberate policy, but is also rendered possible by a number of significant industry features.

1.   The market for pharmaceuticals and its different segments

Specific products are required to treat specific illnesses. Most pharmaceuticals are suitable only for a few purposes, and the market is therefore divided into a number of largely self-contained sectors. The responses of individuals to particular drugs vary greatly. Side-effects are possible and sometimes serious. Within each therapeutic category a choice of alternatives is thought desirable.

The number of drugs marketed is therefore large. In a typical developed country, about one thousand physiologically active compounds will be in use, incorporated into several thousand mixtures and dosage forms (3). Dosage levels are small, however, and the national consumption of most drugs is measured in kilograms rather than tons. Unit value is correspondingly high: in the United Kingdom, for example, 1980 exports of finished drugs were worth about $20 000 per ton compared to $800 per ton for bulk thermoplastics.

Independent of this vertical division by therapeutic class, pharmaceuticals may be divided horizontally into three broad groups according to their technological content.

The first group are the <u>over-the-counter</u> (OTC) drugs, which are sold in most countries directly to consumers without prescription, and with the help of heavy advertising. Competition in this segment of the industry turns largely on the marketing of established brands. New products are rare, and are usually mere reformulations of existing drugs. Proprietary drugs are therefore characterised by high advertising intensities, but low research intensities. Sales have grown more slowly than those of other pharmaceuticals, but nevertheless make up about 15 per cent of the total for the OECD countries (4).

The second group are <u>generic</u> or <u>multisource</u> drugs, out-of-patent products made by more than one company, and available on prescription. They may be sold under brand-names or under their generic name. Price competition is often fierce and profit margins low. Multisource drugs accounted for 45 per cent of all prescription drug sales in the USA in 1979; in Europe they are rather less important but probably have about 20-25 per cent of the market (5). As with OTC products, there is considerable participation by small non-innovative firms, many of whom sell only to domestic or regional markets.

The third group, and the most important as far as this report is concerned, are <u>in-patent drugs</u> sold on prescription. Products of this type are responsible for the spectacular growth of the pharmaceutical industry since the 1930s, and are the ultimate source of prosperity not merely for the innovative company, but for the generic sector as well. Competition is by the development of new forms of chemotherapy. Given patent protection, successful firms are in principle able to earn large returns. The investment required is high, however, and only a limited number of firms are able to participate.

The <u>first</u> and <u>second</u> segments of the market provide a basis for a profitable industry, even in countries where there are no firms with the size, capital and innovative capacity needed to compete in the <u>third</u> segment. Competition in the first two sectors also has an indirect but important influence on the innovative companies. Many generic products started as patented innovations of considerable value, which is why they are still worth making after patent protection has expired. The extent to which the original innovator can retain a market after his patent ends must obviously affect his cash flow and his ability to invest in research.

There are other factors which must be taken into account in analysing the overall market for drugs. In a given country the pattern of demand is determined to a large extent by the incidence of particular diseases and by traditions of medical practice. There are often considerable variations in the type, number and forms of the drugs consumed between one nation and another. As far as dosage forms are concerned, markets tend to be national rather than international in character. This situation is reinforced by variations in health care systems and in government regulation of the admission and pricing of drugs.

2.   <u>The operations of the industry</u>

<u>Innovation</u>

Since the mid-30s, the pharmaceutical industry has been characterised by a high level of research-based innovation. The introduction of new drugs is the major driving force of the industry. The nature of the research and development process and of innovation, and the factors affecting these processes are discussed in detail in Chapter IV. In this overview of the industry's operations, the analysis is limited to some general features.

Product innovation is difficult and therefore expensive. Compounds must be selected for a particular use, extracted or synthesised, and tested for physiological activity. Those which seem suitable are subjected to prolonged and increasingly elaborate trials in animals and later humans to determine their safety and efficacy. Failure is possible at any point, and the chances of success are not high.

As Chapter IV will show, both the time and money required to develop a new drug have risen sharply since 1960. The threshold expenditure for successful product innovation is now high and the large company at a marked advantage. Other forms of innovation, although demanding, are less prodigal of resources. New routes to existing compounds, and new forms of administering known drugs are rather cheaper to develop, and are within the capabilities of more firms.

Production

The production of drugs involves two basic stages: the preparation of the physiologically active ingredients, and their conversion into the forms in which they may be taken.

The active compounds may be extracted from animal or vegetable sources, prepared by fermentation, or synthesised by chemical means. The processes used are generally complex, and require careful control if products of acceptable activity and purity are to be obtained. Substantial economies of scale are possible. The usual relationships between capacity and capital cost apply, and the limiting factor is the need to maintain operating flexibility as production runs are small.

The active substances are then mixed with other ingredients to make them more easily administered, converted into pills, solutions and other forms, and packed for retail distribution. These operations are straightforward in nature, although the work itself is exacting. Once again, economies of scale are possible, although they are less marked than in the manufacture of the active ingredients.

These stages of production do not require the same resources, nor indeed need they be carried out by the same organisation. Moreover, since the volumes involved are small, transport costs are low. A degree of decentralisation, especially of the later processes, is quite practicable. The active material may be made at one site, converted into a bulk mixture at a second, and that mixture divided into dosage units and packed at a third. There is however a point -- which may have been reached some time ago -- at which segmented domestic markets and the decentralisation of downstream operations will have an effect on the price of drugs.

Marketing

In all developed and most developing countries delivery of medical care is largely decentralised, and the majority of doctors practice singly or in small groups. The professional value system emphasises autonomy and the right of the doctor to prescribe whatever he thinks best for the patient. To the drug company the doctor is therefore the customer, and the aim of marketing is to persuade him to favour one product rather than another. This is best achieved by personal contact, and all firms maintain large forces of highly trained salesmen for this purpose. This is the more important as doctors generally rely on the drug company personnel for news of developments in therapies.

Marketing costs for prescription drugs are therefore heavy. Marketing OTC drugs is also expensive, although in this field the major cost is general advertising, which takes place in many countries on television.

3. National markets and production by multinational enterprises

The features of manufacturing and marketing which have just been described explain why every country can build some degree of industrial capacity in pharmaceuticals. These features render multinational operations a feasible, and even to a large extent, a rational proposition. Once oligopoly and extensive government regulations are added to complete the picture (the latter including the advantages often offered by governments to firms accepting to produce domestically), it is easy to understand why large firms have been led to choose to operate through direct foreign investment and manufacturing operations from plant in foreign domestic markets. This mode of operation has allowed them to overcome up to now the drawbacks stemming from the extensive segmentation of national markets. Over the last thirty years production from delocated plant has become a central feature of the industry.

a) The multinational system of operation

At first sight the pharmaceutical industry does not appear as highly concentrated as many others. Overall market concentration in any given country and, indeed, world-wide is relatively low. No single firm has as much as 5 per cent of the world market or 20 per cent of any major national market. The industry, however, is one where a more disaggregated analysis is required.

Since few pharmaceutical products are appropriate to the treatment of more than a limited range of medical conditions, the market for pharmaceuticals is divided into a number of largely self-contained sectors. Within these submarkets, a much higher degree of concentration is frequent. It is common for the submarket leader to account for more than 40 per cent of total sales in that particular field and for the top four companies to account for more than 80 per cent. This degree of concentration is sufficient to ensure firms a dominant market position in submarkets. Instances of anti-trust proceedings by national authorities or in North America or in Europe by the EEC indicate that this market power is often considerable and may lead to abuses.

12

More generally competition between large firms is waged, as is often the case in situations of oligopoly, through product innovation and marketing ability rather than price. In conjunction with the factors discussed above, oligopolistic competition has led large firms, for many decades, to employ a substantial sales force in every country where potential sales are appreciable. Local factors are of outstanding importance in marketing. Health care systems and traditions of medical practive vary. Effective marketing is only possible where these national characteristics are recognised and exploited. Such operations are now invariably organised on a national basis.

This strategy can be taken a step further and extended to the establishment of plants domestically for the formulation and packaging of products. As indicated above, there are few technical barriers to the decentralisation of final drug production. Local formulation and packaging is a very common practice in the industry. A typical average-sized multinational, with world-wide sales of $800 million in 1980, reported that it had 11 such plants in as many countries. A large multinational, with sales of $1 200 million, had 39 in 38 countries. The reasons for this strategy are many and varied. It is often convenient to satisfy special local requirements of form or packaging by local production, especially if the market is large. Some companies consider that doctors are more ready to prescribe a product if it is made locally. In some countries government regulations for admission of drugs on the market are easier to meet if products are manufactured locally. The report returns to this point in Chapter V.

The production of the pharmacologically active ingredients is normally confined to a much more limited range of centres than is formulation and packaging. Representative figures are difficult to obtain but scattered evidence suggests that even large companies may have only two or three such plants and more than six is uncommon. These establishments are usually sited in developed countries and most commonly in the parent companies' home country, or where the tax situation is especially favourable.

The general view, within the industry, is that at this stage of the production process, economies of scale are of real importance. Chemical production requires a higher level of skill and training than formulation and packaging, and is best carried out in countries with a fully developed technical and economic infrastructure. Restrictions on the import of fine chemicals are generally much less severe than those on finished pharmaceuticals. These factors favour centralised large-scale production in the parent country or in a limited number of advanced countries.

Research is generally the most centralised activity in a multinational pharmaceutical company. Even very large firms only carry out serious research at a handful of locations. None of the first 25 has more than eight centres of research and most have substantially fewer. Usually, one or two are much larger than the rest and frequently a single group of laboratories accounts for 80 per cent or more of the total effort.

The main centre of research is normally in the firm's country of origin, and other important establishments are placed in nations with a proven record of success in innovation. American companies have taken the lead in

13

Table 1

LOCAL PRODUCTION OF DRUGS BY THE AFFILIATES OF FOREIGN COMPANIES
COMPARED TO DIRECT IMPORTS BY SELECTED COUNTRIES
(1980)

| Country | Consumption ($ Million) | Source (%) | | | Ratio of Foreign-Owned Local Prodution to Direct Imports |
		Made by Locally-Owned Companies	Made Locally by Foreign-Owned Companies	Direct Imports	
Austria	430	20	24	56	0.4
Belgium	780	13	30	57	0.25
Denmark	215	42	n.a.	58	
Finland	240	60	n.a.	40	
France	4 950	47	50	3	15.7
Germany	5 050	65	20	15	1.3
Greece	440	62	15	23	0.6
Italy	3 200	44	48	8	6.0
Netherlands	580	24	5	71	0.1
Portugal	350	34	35	31	1.0
Spain	1 950	39	58	3	19.0
Sweden	530	49	n.a.	51	
Switzerland	580	39	n.a.	61	
United Kingdom	2 150	46	38	16	2.4
United States	12 610	81	17	2	8.5
Canada	950	27	63	10	6.3
Australia	530			15	
Japan	13 150	86	10	4	2.5
Developing countries	11 500	26	49	25	2.0
World (1)	61 000	60	27	13	2.1

1. Excluding CMEA and the People's Republic of China.
n.a. = not available.

Source : See Annex.

14

setting up a second research centre abroad, in part for reasons of managerial efficiency, and in part because of the particularly restrictive approach adopted by the FDA from the mid-60s onwards.

b) The balance between exports and local production of MNEs

This multinational mode of operation has aided large firms to overcome existing obstacles to the world-wide export of products and to recover the high and continually rising costs of research and development on a world basis despite the fragmentation of national markets. Multinational operations have offered an effective way to penetrate national markets. Table 1 shows the importance of foreign direct investment in this respect. World-wide, about twice the value of finished drugs are made by the local affiliates of transnational companies as are exchanged across national frontiers. This is true both of developed and developing countries. The evolution of the pattern of world trade has been deeply and durably influenced by this feature of the industry.

The balance between exports and local production by foreign affiliates varies a great deal from country to country. In Europe, for example, the output of foreign-owned companies is of major importance in France, Italy, Spain and the United Kingdom, and is significant in Germany and in Belgium. Elsewhere it plays a minor part. The Netherlands and the Nordic countries only encounter the multinationals as distributors. Canada, Australia and the developing nations depend heavily on the foreign firms to which they are host, Japan and the USA much less so.

American companies have adopted the transnational form of operation widely and systematically. These firms typically make far more finished drugs in local factories scattered throughout the world than they dispatch from the United States (6). Recent data suggest that the ratio of finished drugs produced abroad to direct exports is as high as 12:1 for US companies. It is significant that, unlike any other major country, the USA exports far more intermediates than finished drugs. The same is true, though not to the same extent, of the principal Swiss companies. World-wide sales of the three principal Swiss companies were about $4 500 million in 1980, of which $350 million were in Switzerland. Swiss exports totalled $1 600 million, which suggests that production abroad was around $2 500 million. In Germany, direct exports and local production abroad are of comparable importance, while the major UK and French firms rely more on the exports.

4. National capacities for innovation

The factors which have been analysed above mean that many countries, and all those of the OECD, possess a pharmaceutical industry of one kind or another. Their ability to perform particular activities varies widely, however. In terms of their capacity for innovation and their ability to develop and market high-technology products, nations may be divided into three groups:

Table 2

THE PHARMACEUTICAL BALANCE OF TRADE AND NATIONAL CAPACITY IN 1980
in $ Million

Country	Capacity for innovation	Production	Balance in Finished Drugs (1)	Balance in Intermediates (2)	Overall Trade Balance (1 + 2)
Austria	Low	390	-121	-26	-147
Belgium	Medium	850	101	-87	14
Denmark	Medium	450	112	-10	102
Finland	Low	196	-72	-12	-84
France	High	5 950	1 008	-212	796
Germany	High	8 405	628	353	981
Ireland	Low	175	-53	62	9
Italy	Medium	3 950	54	-20	34
Netherlands	Medium	775	-24	51	27
Portugal	Low	300	-86	-40	-126
Spain	Low	2 350	29	-112	-83
Sweden	Medium	570	-15	-6	-21
Switzerland	High	2 400	794	410	1 204
United Kingdom	High	4 150	886	322	1 208
United States	High	16 150	402	831	1 233
Canada	Low	1 150	-57	-185	-242
Australia	Low	620	-44	-31	-75
Japan	High	15 500	-468	-312	-780
Developing countries	Low	9 500	-2 500	-1 010	-3 510

Source : See Annex.

16

i) High capacity countries: these are nations which have a strong complement of large diversified pharmaceutical companies and a history of achievement in innovation. They are the homes of the world's leading multinational firms, and are the main diffusers of pharmaceutical technology outside their national boundaries;

ii) Medium capacity countries: these countries have a few large national drug companies. Most indigenous firms, however, are undiversified and have only a moderate capacity for innovation. Most product or process development tends to be imitative. The national companies may have a large export capacity, but usually engage in foreign investment or technology transfer to a limited extent. Certain of them, however, have a strong international position in other fields and, under the appropriate circumstances, could bring the domestically owned part of the industry into the high-capacity group;

iii) Low capacity countries: these nations have small undiversified local enterprises whose activities are largely imitative. Their pharmaceutical industry is dominated by foreign multinational companies. The prospects of developing an indigenous pharmaceutical sector, actively engaged in international operations, are very limited.

Table 2 gives a general indication of the capacity, production and trade balance in pharmaceuticals of Member countries in 1980.

Chapter III

THE PATTERN OF INTERNATIONAL TRADE

No nation is completely self-sufficient in drugs, although several approach this position. Many cannot make much of what they need: as has already been emphasised, capacities are unequally distributed. In the advanced segment, the technology of the industry also encourages trade. There are large economies of scale both in innovation and in some key phases of manufacture. New products, a major form of competition, are extremely expensive to develop, and must be sold world-wide to recover their costs. International trade is one reponse to this necessity, even if foreign direct investment has become one of the industry's most characteristic ways of achieving world-wide sales.

1. The structure of world trade

A bird's-eye view of 1980 world trade in finished pharmaceuticals and in intermediate products is shown in Figures 1 and 2. A more detailed breakdown is given in Annex Tables A3 to A7.

The value of the trade was nearly $14 000 million, of which a little under $8 000 million was in the form of finished drugs, and almost $6 000 million in the form of raw materials and intermediates (7). It is clear from Figure 1 that the trade in finished pharmaceuticals is very largely between the countries of Western Europe and from Western Europe to the Third World. Despite their immense output and consumption of finished drugs, the USA and Japan both import and export relatively small amounts of such products, and in this sense may fairly be described as self-contained. The other non-European developed nations are in the same position, as is, to an even greater extent, the Eastern bloc. OECD trade with CMEA is about $250 million and with China $7 million. Almost all is in the form of intermediates.

With intermediates the state of affairs is more complex. Here the role of the USA is strikingly more important, as Table 2 and Figure 2 show. Although accounting for a mere 9 per cent of world exports of finished drugs, it provides 23 per cent of all exports of intermediates, and has a trade surplus with all its partners on this account. Part of these exports are made between US parent companies and their affiliates abroad. Japan is a substantial net importer, as are Canada, Australia and South Africa. About one-third of the trade for intermediates is within Europe, which, taken as a whole, has a negative balance with the USA, but a large surplus with the developing countries.

18

Figure 1

THE STRUCTURE OF WORLD TRADE IN FINISHED DRUGS, 1980,
(EXCLUDING CMEA AND CHINA)
(BASE 1 000)[1]

From / To	OECD Europe	USA	Japan	Other developed	Developing countries	Total
OECD Europe	467	31	1	2	1	502
USA	19		3	1	5	28
Japan	45	12		1		58
Other developed	28	12			3	43
Developing countries	314	35		1	18	368
Total	873	90	4	8	24	1 000

Figure 2

THE STRUCTURE OF WORLD TRADE IN INTERMEDIATES, 1980
(EXCLUDING CMEA AND CHINA)
(BASE 1 000)[1]

From / To	OECD Europe	USA	Japan	Other ceveloped	Developing countries	Total
OECD Europe	350	117	8	6	25	506
USA	48		9	2	10	69
Japan	29	41			22	92
Other developed	24	21	10			55
Developing countries	162	49		10	57	278
Total	613	228	27	18	114	1 000

Source : See Notes and Tables in Annex.

1. In Figures 1-4 total trade figures are taken, as appropriate, from Tables A-5 and A-6, and have been converted so as to add up to 1 000. Trade between particular countries or areas is then expressed as a proportion of this total.

2.   The situation in Europe

Intra-European trade in pharmaceuticals presents a complex polycentric pattern which is shown in Figures 3 and 4.

Most European Member countries import a substantial proportion of the finished drugs that they consume. In Germany and the United Kingdom imports are about 15 per cent of the total, but in the smaller nations of Central and Northern Europe they range from 40 up to 76 per cent. This behaviour is not, however, universal. France, Italy and Spain are largely self-sufficient, and for their size Portugal and Greece import less than might be expected. As far as exports to other European countries are concerned, Germany is dominant, followed at some distance by Switzerland, the United Kingdom, France and Belgium. Italy, Spain and Portugal export little in the way of finished drugs.

A further look at the structure of trade suggests that not only competitive strength in pharmaceuticals, but also general commercial and cultural ties are important. For example, Germany trades extensively with Austria, Belgium, Italy and Switzerland. Similarly, the Scandinavian countries trade extensively with each other and also have close links with the United Kingdom and the Netherlands.

The pattern of intra-European trade in intermediates is generally similar to that in finished drugs. Interdependence, is, however, much more marked and no country can be described as self-contained. Germany, Switzerland, the United Kingdom and Italy are the largest exporters, and the first three of these countries enjoy a positive balance of payments on this account. All others, including France, are in substantial deficit. As previously noted, there is a large trade in intermediates with the USA, which is much in favour of the latter.

3.   Trade with the developing countries

The developing countries import both finished drugs and intermediates on a large scale. Their own exports are limited in value, and consist mainly of raw materials and simple active compounds. The export trade of developing countries is difficult however to estimate with preciseness, since several of them have an extensive business as general entrepots. Singapore, Hong Kong and, to a lesser extent, Korea export antibiotics and other active materials, mainly to Japan.

As Figure A1 (see Annex) shows, the large developing country markets for finished drugs are Africa and the OPEC nations of the Middle East. In both areas imports form a high proportion of consumption and the local industries are weak or non-existent. By contrast the countries of East Asia and Central and South America carry out the later stages of manufacture themselves and are relatively self-sufficient in finished products. They are however still heavily dependent on imports of active ingredients.

The supply of finished drugs to the Third World is dominated by Europe and, in particular, by France, Germany, Switzerland and the United Kingdom. As far as intermediates are concerned, these countries are joined by Italy and, above all, by the USA (cf. Figure A2). It is clear that the commercial

20

Figure 3

THE STRUCTURE OF INTRA-EUROPEAN TRADE IN FINISHED DRUGS, 1980 (BASE 1 000)[1]

To \ From	Germany	Switzerland	UK	France	Belgium	Netherlands	Italy	Spain and Portugal	Scandinavia	Other	Total
Germany		39	25	39	33	15	13	2	16	17	200
Switzerland	25		6	13	6	4	3	2	6	3	64
United Kingdom	24	11		9	5	6	2		14	8	79
France	6	4	9		7	7	5	4	4	1	47
Belgium	34	16	10	24		3	2	1	11	3	95
Netherlands	21	8	11	11	40				3	5	107
Italy	29	14	6	8	8	6			3	3	79
Scandinavia	28	20	29	3	12	16	3	1	44	1	158
Spain and Portugal	6	13	7	1	3	3	1		3	3	39
Other	44	21	35	5	6	7	3	1	8		132
Total	217	146	138	113	120	67	32	10	113	44	1 000

Figure 4

THE STRUCTURE OF INTRA-EUROPEAN TRADE IN INTERMEDIATES, 1980 (BASE 1 000)[1]

To \ From	Germany	Switzerland	UK	France	Belgium	Netherlands	Italy	Spain and Portugal	Scandinavia	Other	Total
Germany		29	13	22	7	29	18	10	4	18	181
Switzerland	48		9	12	2	2	28	3	4	5	91
United Kingdom	13	1		5	3	5		4	4	2	37
France	41	42	17		16	12	32	3	9	7	179
Belgium	12	7	12	13		4	13	3	5	6	72
Netherlands	17	3	21	9	4		6	4	5	3	72
Italy	44	32	22	11	2	8		2	4	3	128
Scandinavia	27	8	10	4	5	2	2	2	10	3	73
Spain and Portugal	21	21	13	14	5	1	6			11	92
Other	27	11	11	4	9	2	7	1	1		73
Total	231	173	140	94	53	65	111	32	43	58	1 000

Source: As for Figures 1 and 2.

1. See explanation under Figure 2.

21

ties formed in colonial times remain strong. This is especially the case with France, for whom exports to French-speaking African States make up nearly 40 per cent of her total trade. Likewise Britain dominates the trade in drugs with English-speaking African countries, as does Belgium that with Zaire. Portugal has a strong presence in Angola and Mozambique, and Spain in South America.

4.   The evolution of trade and changes in export shares

During the past twenty years world trade in drugs has increased from perhaps 12 per cent of output to about 16 per cent. Its nature has also changed.

During this period the proportion of intra-OECD pharmaceuticals rose from 51 per cent to 68 per cent. In particular, there has been a steady increase in trade between the European countries. Imports of finished drugs rose from 6 per cent to 15 per cent of consumption during this period. A similar trend in the trade in intermediates is also evident. All developed countries, even those which are largely self-sufficient, have shared this tendency towards increased interdependence to some extent.

The experience of the developing world has been complementary. For them, imports have become relatively less important. This is especially so with finished drugs, where imports were about 50 per cent of consumption in 1960 compared to only 25 per cent in 1980. In line with the trend towards increased local production, intermediates have formed a growing proportion of imports and now make up about one-third of the total.

As far as the major exporters are concerned, the most striking development of the past twenty years has been the sharp decline of the USA. Its share of the world trade in finished drugs fell from 29 per cent in 1960 to 15 per cent in 1970, where it has remained. This reflects two different sets of factors: firstly, as in so many other industries, the other advanced nations have caught up, and, secondly, the major American companies have universally adopted a multinational strategy. Western Europe increased its share from 56 to 75 per cent, with Germany and the smaller countries improving their relative position.

5.   Trade and national capacities for innovation

These facts suggest certain conclusions. With few exceptions, the countries of high capacity, as defined in Chapter II.4 above, take the bulk of the export trade. Conversely, the nations of low capacity have only a minor share, with those of intermediate strength coming somewhere in between.

The picture is considerably more complex on the import side. Foreign direct investment, often rendered necessary and in some cases actually encouraged by government measures, represents a major factor shaping the pattern of imports. Thus it is not useful, in many instances, to consider the imports of finished drugs by countries separately from that of their imports of intermediates.

As Tables A5 and A6 in Annex show, imports of finished drugs, whatever their relative importance, come mainly from the countries of high capacity. Imports of intermediates are also largely from such countries, although Ireland and certain developing nations are more important as exporters of intermediates than might be expected. The reasons for this anomaly are explained below.

Chapter IV

INNOVATION, TECHNOLOGICAL CAPACITIES, LICENSING AND CO-OPERATION IN R&D

The high-technology products of the pharmaceutical industry come from the patented drug sector. It is there that innovation is central to investment and profits. If trade related issues are also to be examined in the light of their direct or indirect effects on the process of innovation and the funds available for investment in R&D, the main features of this process must now be considered.

1.   Trends in the output and cost of innovation

The innovative segment of the pharmaceutical industry is highly intensive in R&D. Average annual expenditure on R&D represents between 8 per cent and 10 per cent of sales and for some firms it is much higher. One specific feature of the industry is the high rate of spending on basic research: US data indicate that it is well above 10 per cent of total R&D outlays.

Basic research is an on-going activity in large firms. Once a new substance has been discovered, the process of development involves three main phases: the synthesis of active materials and the establishment of their biological effects; extensive biological testing in animals and later humans to determine pharmacological activity and detect adverse effects; and finally product development. This process is lengthy, costly and uncertain. In the early stages of a major project hundreds of chemicals will be examined, of which only a handful will be selected for serious investigation in animals. Perhaps only two of the latter will subsequently be tested in humans. Most compounds will fail to show therapeutic advantages or will not be commercially promising. On average, two to four years will elapse from the selection of a potential candidate to the start of clinical trials.

In all developed countries trials on human beings must be conducted according to carefully specified and officially approved methods which differ to some extent from country to country (see Chapter V below). In the USA where the requirements are particularly elaborate, clinical testing begins in healthy volunteers and moves first to small and then to larger samples of patients. New products are subjected to a first screening by the United States Food and Drug Administration (FDA) and classified on this basis as first class and totally new, as good as the ones which already exist or finally as "me too products" not up to common standards. Although the final phase of the new drug approval procedure has been considerably speeded up for the drugs recognised early in the process as belonging to the first category, the average time required for drug approval in the US is currently more than eight years. This is an extreme case, but periods required for testing are now prolonged in most countries. In many countries, moreover, post-marketing surveillance is now required for all new drugs.

However, while the strong R&D basis of pharmaceutical production must be stressed, some product innovation undertaken by firms is not highly original. As is suggested by the FDA classification, innovation may consist in finding new routes to slightly modified versions of highly successful drugs produced by competitors. It also comprises the development of what the profession designates as "me too products". Since new drug approval is required for all products which claim to be novel, this factor must be taken into account when considering the length of procedures or the number of products approved.

In pharmaceuticals as in other industrial activities, the output from research is not easy to quantify. Patent statistics are an inherently unreliable guide: a patent may relate to a major or a trivial discovery. The number of new pharmaceutical agents or new chemical entitities (NCEs) introduced to the market is a somewhat more sensitive index of innovative activity, but gives little weight to novelty and none to commercial success. The enumeration of medically or commercially outstanding products necessarily involves a choice of indicators which may vary from expert to expert.

The most commonly used indicator is the introduction of new chemical entities. Figures for the USA are shown in Table 3, from which it is clear that after a sharp fall in the early 60s, innovative output has been fairly steady between 1963 and 1980. Similar trends have been observed in the major European countries. Statistics of published papers and of patents suggest that innovative activity has perhaps increased during this period, even if it has not been reflected in the introduction of new products to the market.

Table 3

US APPROVED NCEs, BY NATIONALITY (OWNERSHIP) OF INNOVATING COMPANY
1951-1980

Time Interval	Number of NCEs	United States		Foreign	
		Origin	Percentage	Origin	Percentage
1951-56	172	109	63	63	37
1957-62	188	109	58	79	42
1963-68	88	53	60	35	40
1969-74	76	37	49	39	51
1975-80	94	54	57	40	43

Source: Center for Study of Drug Development, University of Rochester, reproduced in The Competitive Status of the US Pharmaceutical Industry, National Academy Press, Washington, D.C., 1983.

The cost and time required for the development of new drugs has unquestionably risen sharply during the past 20 years. In constant value, the money required per NCE reaching the market has been estimated at $6.5 million before 1962 compared to $45 million in 1980 exclusive of capital expenditure. There is reason to believe that the latter figure is too low rather than too high (8). Development times have risen from 3-5 years in the early 60s to 9-12 years or even longer today.

Two factors explain this increase in the cost of innovation. First, the disease areas currently attracting attention -- circulatory problems, cancers, psychotic illnesses -- require a detailed understanding of the mechanisms involved if adequate forms of treatment are to be developed. Highly specialised medical, biological and biochemical skills are required. Secondly, substantially more extensive clinical trials and toxicological testing are needed before a new product can be marketed. Advances in medical science have made it possible to identify a much larger range of potentially adverse reactions than was previously the case.

At the same time the progress of knowledge has made it possible to predict the physiological effects of compounds with much greater ease. This reduces the time and money required to develop a new product. The costs of innovation have undoubtedly risen, but had it not been for the advancement of basic science they would have done so to an even greater extent. Further developments of this type may be anticipated, and those expected as a result of biotechnology are discussed below.

The increase in cost of innovation has serious consequences for the medium-sized company, and for the country whose capacity for innovation is embodied in such firms. There is now a very high threshold of research spending below which a company has little chance of developing a genuinely novel product. In 1980 this threshold was probably about $25 million per year, corresponding to annual sales of around $200 -- 250 million. A major firm would expect to spend $100 million or more. Today dramatic increases in the cost of innovation probably represent the strongest single factor increasing concentration in the pharmaceutical industry. Small and medium innovative enterprises cease to be viable because of the increasing cost of innovation and are absorbed by larger firms or pull out of drug development. As discussed below, such firms may also have increasing difficulties in obtaining licences as internationalisation develops.

2.   The nature of national scientific and technological capacities

Historically, the development of a high capacity for pharmaceutical innovation depended to a considerable extent on factors outside the industry. These factors allowed companies located in certain countries to seize the opportunities of the 1930s and 1940s and have helped them to maintain their position ever since. The most important of these were a substantial domestic market, general strength in chemical technology, and a large and active scientific community.

Today, however, these factors are necessary rather than sufficient. As has already been emphasized, the capacity for innovation is primarily located in firms, and the national capacity of a country is manifested through the companies based on its soil. The cost and complexity of the innovation process favour firms compared to other types of institutions.

However important they are at the level of fundamental research, universities and government research laboratories have been only a minor source of actual pharmaceutical products. Universities are sources of fundamental background knowledge and of informed and critical expertise on technical problems. National centres of medical research play a similar role. Hospitals, of course, are intimately associated with the process of clinical testing.

On account of this, two separate indicators of R&D expenditure are required for assessing national scientific and technological capacities: R&D outlays by firms (see Table 4) and R&D funding for health by governments and universities (see Table 5).

As far as international competitiveness is concerned, the most significant indicators are the level and more particularly still the rate of growth of R&D by firms. The lead times required for innovation in pharmaceuticals mean that today's R&D expenditure is an indicator of relative competitiveness five to ten years from now.

Much of government and university funding for health R&D results in the production of fundamental knowledge which is international rather than national in character and represents a pool from which innovative firms from all countries can draw in many instances quite freely (9). Here again the large company with its world-wide network of scientific contacts and sometimes of laboratories has a decided advantage over the small one.

3. The impact of biotechnology

Biotechnology is defined as "the application of scientific and engineering principles to the processing of materials by biological agents to provide goods and services" (10). In the pharmaceutical context it refers to the production of medicines by these means. Biotechnological processes, notably fermentation processes, have been used for many years in the drug industry to make, among other products, antibiotics, steroids, enzymes and vaccines. Since about eight years the potential importance of biotechnology has suddenly increased dramatically. This has been mainly due to the development of genetic engineering, notably in the area of relevance to pharmaceuticals, of in vitro recombinant DNA technology.

There is a general consensus in the pharmaceutical industry today that the new biotechnology may have -- from the late 1980s onwards -- an effect comparable to the therapeutic revolution of the 1930s and 40s. Three main areas of application are being exploited:

Table 4

DOMESTIC R&D OUTLAYS BY FIRMS IN THE PHARMACEUTICAL INDUSTRY IN SELECTED OECD COUNTRIES (1967-1980) (a)
(in 1975 million US dollars)

	1967	1973	1975	1980	Growth rate 1967-1980
High capacity countries (b)					
United States	548.8	827.7	981.0	1 241.7	7.1
Japan	115.9	282.1	320.7	515.4	12.1
France	136.7(c)	172.5	188.5	261.0	6.4(g)
United Kingdom	79.2	145.0(d)	174.2	292.6(e)	9.7(h)
Medium capacity countries					
Italy	59.6	103.0	105.0	132.7	6.3
Sweden	28.5	46.3	47.0	77.2(f)	11.7(i)
Belgium	16.5	27.0	35.6	47.7(f)	12.1(i)

(a) The standardised form for collecting business enterprise R&D expenditure established by the Frascati Manual is that of gross domestic expenditures. This includes R&D expenditure made abroad by affiliates of multinational enterprises, but also includes the outlays made in the country considered by foreign affiliates.
(b) Germany and Switzerland do not report to OECD their business enterprise R&D outlays for pharmaceuticals.
(c) 1970.   (d) 1972.   (e) 1981.   (f) 1979.   (g) 1970-80.   (h) 1967-81.   (i) 1967-79.

Source : OECD, Science and Technology Indicators Unit.

Table 5

DATA ON GOVERNMENT FUNDING OF R&D FOR HEALTH IN SELECTED
HIGH CAPACITY OECD COUNTRIES IN 1979

	United States	Japan	Germany	France	United Kingdom
Health R&D in million dollars	3 524	130	247	209	78
Health R&D per capita population (in dollars)					
Health (a)	14	1	3	3	1
Health + Medical Science (b)	14	2	4	3	4
Health + Medical Science + University Medical Research (c)	17 (d)	6	11	7	4
Health + Medical Science + University Medical Research (c) as a percentage of all government outlays for health	7.5 (d)	2.1	2.4	2.1	1.5

(a) Government health expenditure stricto sensu.
(b) Health plus the direct medical science content of Advancement of Knowledge.
(c) Health, medical science plus university medical research financed indirectly by general university funds.
(d) Total health-related R&D funded by federal government.

Source : Trends in Science and Technology in the OECD Area during the 1970s: Resources Devoted to R&D, Science and Technology Indicators Unit, OECD, Paris, 1982, Tables 2.18 and 2.20.

a) The improvement of existing biotechnological processes in order to obtain higher yields and purer products;

b) The development of routes to materials of high therapeutic value which are otherwise inaccessible, such as human insulin, human growth hormone and interferon;

c) The introduction of entirely new materials, such as novel antibiotics, vaccines and diagnostic agents.

A notable feature of this development has been the part played by highly specialised small firms which are tiny compared to the typical world-scale drug company. Almost without exception, as will be seen below, these firms are linked to the large ones by contracts, licensing agreements and often ownership. The reasons are obvious. The early stages of innovation are relatively cheap, but safety testing and product development need resources far beyond a specialised research organisation. A symbiotic relationship with the large companies has been the answer.

As far as the distribution of national capacities for pharmaceutical innovation is concerned, it seems probable that the effect of these developments will be to reinforce the position of those countries which are already dominant. As in previous therapeutic revolutions, they alone have the human and organisational resources to seize the opportunities which biotechnology offers. The Japanese lead in certain fields of biotechnology and the rapid growth of their business enterprise R&D (see Table 4), may well result in Japan showing much greater competitivity than in the past.

The future of the upper tier of large innovative multinational enterprises (see Table A8 in Annex) also seems assured, although the growth of one or more of the new research firms into something bigger cannot be excluded. At present, however, vertical specialisation seems to be the most common adaptation to the new developments.

4. International licensing and scientific and technological co-operation between firms

In 1977-78, interviews with the leading pharmaceutical companies suggested that the availability of technology in the form of licensing agreements was becoming limited, in particular for operations in European countries. Owing to the increased difficulty in developing new drugs, firms appeared increasingly reluctant to share their findings with other companies and tended to retain the full control of production of their patented products. Some of the larger companies indicated that they had reserves of technology which they might use for licensing in a later period, but that these exchanges would tend to take the form of "swap" agreements with other firms rather than outright sales (11).

The OECD study found that most multinational firms co-operated with one or more of their counterparts in product markets. While this generally entailed licensing agreements which enabled the licensed firms to produce pharmaceuticals which they would not otherwise produce, co-operation between firms could extend to the use of intermediates, product development and even research into drug discovery (although this was exceptional at the time).

The extent to which firms internationalise their operations also appears to have a direct bearing on their readiness to grant licences to foreign firms. In countries where large foreign firms have set up production plants, it is often impossible for smaller firms to acquire licences. Licensing remains important for medium (or sometimes larger) companies, in instances where they lack the financial strength to invest directly in an important market. It may also represent a transition phase prior to direct investment. These factors explain why the number of licensing agreements for production on the US market made between medium, and even moderately large, European companies and small American companies increased over the past fifteen years at a time when the number of intra-European agreements were diminishing.

The rising cost of R&D and the deteriorating situation of small innovative pharmaceutical firms explain the great interest with which the emergence of the small genetic engineering firms has been observed. These firms are not part of the pharmaceutical industry, although they have close links with it.

A report made by the US Office of Technological Assessment (OTA) has noted that "genetic engineering is not in itself an industry, but a technology used at the laboratory level" (12). This is a useful insight which helps to explain why the highly specialised firms in this area may be seen as:

i) performing a particular phase of R&D and product and process development, within a wider industrial framework into which they are integrated by a wide variety of contractual agreements; and

ii) offering major firms from different technologically-related branches of industry and different countries, a novel way of achieving co-operation in R&D by purchasing equity or funding basic research and product development contracts in these companies.

Major pharmaceutical, petrochemical and chemical firms have helped to set up, or increase the capital of, the specialised genetic engineering firms, and have either signed research contracts or established more elaborate forms of industrial cooperation for the development and production of given products. A sample of the two forms of relations established with the best known genetic engineering firms is given in Figure 5. The pharmaceutical firms involved are generally large innovation-based multinational enterprises.

Many of the agreements are international. Japanese firms have been particularly interested in establishing ties with the specialised US genetic engineering enterprises. A sample of Japanese-US agreements is given in Figure 6.

Figure 5

SELECTED GENETIC ENGINEERING FIRMS WITH MAIN INVESTORS AND CONTRACTS (1982)

Firms	Headquarters	Date of establ.	Personnel	Main outside investors	Firms having signed R&D, product development or manufacturing contracts
Biogen	Geneva (Switz) and Cambridge, Mass. (USA)	1978	180	International Nickel Schering Plough Monsanto Grand Metropolitan	International Nickel (mineral leaching) Schering Plough (interferon) Green Cross (antigen for hepatitis B) Novo (human insulin) Shionogi (huan albumin serum) International Minerals & Chemicals (animal growth hormones) Meiji Seika (antibiotics manuf. processes)
Biologicals	Toronto (Canada)	1978	100	Allied Chemical Johnson & Johnson Canmont Investment	Stone & Webster (biomass conversion for ethanol Johnson & Johnson (priority for all therapeutical agents) Diamond Shamrock (animal growth hormone) Research Council of Alberta (enzymology) Nisso Shoji (gene synthetiser) Koutron (Hoffman-La Roche) (idem)
Biotech Research Lab.	Rockville Maryland (USA)	1973	50	Ethyl Corp. Fujizoki Pharm.	Ethyl Corp. (microbiological processes) Fujizoki Pharm. (monoclonal antibodies for diagnostics)
Celltech	Slough (UK)	1980	80	British Technology Group Prudential Assurance Midland Bank British and Commonwealth Shipping Technical Development Capital	Agrigenetics (US) (product dev. of genetic material) Shell Sumitomo (monoclonal antibodies)
Cetus	Berkeley, California (USA)	1971	450	Standard Oil of Indiana Socal National Distillers Blyth Eastman Hambrecht and Quist Diebold Venture Ina Corp.	Schering Plough (antibiotics manuf. processes) Roussel Uclaf (manuf. process for B12 vitamin) Social (enzymatic process for fructose manuf.) National Distillers (ethanol process from corn) Standard Oil of Indiana (fermentation processes) Shell (interferon) Smith, Kline & Beckman (vaccines, antigens)
Collaborative Research and Collaborative Genetics	Waltham, Mass. (USA)	1961 1979	125	Dow Chemical Green Cross (Japan)	Sterling Drug (diagnostic agents) Warner Lambert (urokinase) Dow Chemicals (genetic engineering) Akzo Pharma (animal growth hormones) Green Cross (interferon, urokinase)
Enzo Biochem	New York, N.Y. (USA)	1976	50	Johnson & Johnson	Johnson & Johnson (diagnostic agents) Meiji Seika (pregnancy test)
Genentech	South San Francisco California (USA)	1976	350	Lubrizol Fluor Corp. Monsanto Emerson Electric Corning Glass Sun Chemical Kleiner & Perkina Sofinnova	Eli Lilly (human insulin) A.B. Kabi (human growth hormones) Hoffman La Roche (interferon) Daiichi Seiyaku) Toray Ind. ((immun. interferon) Monsanto (animal growth hormones) International Minerals & Chem. Corp. (animal vaccines) Kyowa Hakko) Mitsubishi Chem. ((thrombolytic agent) Corning Glass Works (enzymes for food processing) Gruenthal (urokinase)
Genex	Rockville, Maryland (USA)	1977	200	Koppers Monsanto (par Innoven) Emerson Electric (par Innoven) Johnston Associates	Bristol Myers (interferon) Koppers (mineral leaching) Mitsui Toatsu (urokinase) Green Cross (human albumin serum) Fortia Pharmacia

Source : OECD and DAFSA (cf. Figure 6).

31

Figure 6

R&D CO-OPERATION LICENSING AGREEMENTS AND JOINT VENTURES BETWEEN
JAPANESE AND UNITED STATES FIRMS IN BIOTECHNOLOGY (AS OF MID-1982)

Japanese firms	US Associate	Area of co-operation
Ajinomoto	Charles River Breeding Laboratory	Establishment of the joint venture company, Charles River Japan (genetic engineering for breeding laboratory test animals)
	G.D. Searle	Production of aspartame for Searle
Daiichi Seiyaku	Genentech	R&D contract for interferon
Fujizoki Pharmaceuticals	Biotech Research Lab.	R&D contract for monoclonal antibodies. Investment in Biotech
Green Cross Corp.	Biogen	Licence for manufacturing a vaccin against hepatitis B developed by Biogen
	Bristol Myers	Licence for manufacturing gamma interferon
	Collaborative Research	Investment in collaborative research R&D contract for the manufacture of urokinase
	Genex	R&D contract for the manufacture of human albumin serum
Kyowa Hakko Kogyo	Genentech	R&D contract for an anti-coagulant agent
Meiji Seika	Biogen	R&D contract for improving the manufacture of antibiotics through micro-organisms
	Enzo Biochem	Manufacture of a pregnancy test based on the technology of monoclonal antibodies developed by Enzo Biochem
	G.D. Searle	Agreement for the marketing by Meiji-Seika of interferon developed by Searle
Mitsubishi Chemical	Genentech	R&D contract for an anti coagulant agent
	Hybritech	Marketing of products manufactured by cell culture technology developed by Hybritech
	Monsanto	R&D contract for recombinant genetic engineering and on monoclonal antibodies
Mitsui Toatsu	Genentech	Agreement for the manufacture of interferon
	Genex	Agreement for the manufacture of urokinase
Mochida	G.D. Searle	Licence for the technology of manufacturing interferon through cell fusion
Otsuka Seiyaku	Dow Chemical	Establishment of the joint venture company Otsuka Dow in Japan, which will produce interferon in particular
Shionogi	Biogen	Agreement for the manufacture of human albumin serum and interferon
	Eli Lilly	Agreement for the manufacture of human insulin
Takara Shuzo	Genex	Marketing of synthetic ADN developed by Genex
Toray Industries	Genentech	R&D contract for interferon
Yamanouchi	Genex	R&D contract for fibrine dissolvant
	Revlon	Establishment in Japan of the joint venture company Armour-Yamanouchi for the marketing of immunological products arising from R&D done by Revlon

Source: La biotechnologie dans le monde: stratégies des entreprises et structures industrielles, DAFSA, Paris, 1982, in cooperation with Biofutur.

Chapter V

NATIONAL LEGISLATION AND GOVERNMENT MEASURES

In all countries the pharmaceutical industry is subject to an above average degree of government attention and regulation. This control occurs even in Member countries where government regulation of industry is otherwise weak. It is generally exercised by a variety of agencies and in pursuit of a multiplicity of ends. A Health Ministry will be primarily concerned with the safety and efficacy of drugs, and a Finance Ministry with their cost. A Ministry of Industry may wish to develop the local industry in order to improve the national pharmaceutical capacity, and a Ministry of Trade to reduce a balance of payments deficit. Co-ordinated policies are the exception rather than the rule.

The most widely shared concerns of governments are those related to the safety and efficacy of drugs and to their price. Policies directed towards the development of national capacities for innovation or for production are found in a number of Member countries but not in all. Fewer Member countries still have policies aimed specifically at foreign trade objectives.

As has been noted previously, much of the legislation and these policies have some impact or other, often an important one, on the operations and economics of the industry. To a fairly large extent the overall patterns of international trade and investment which have prevailed over the last thirty years have been the result of longstanding legislation and policies. To the extent that trade related issues exist in this industry, they are not generally recent in origin.

Accordingly this chapter has two objectives. It seeks to identify recent developments which may be having impacts above and beyond those which contributed to the emergence of the structure of trade analysed in Chapter III. It also attempts to indicate areas where harmonization of national legislation and procedures might lead to a reduction of regulatory barriers to trade.

1.   The approval and admission of new drugs

In no country are pharmaceutical companies free to introduce new products without formality. Invariably they are required to register them with the local administration, who must be convinced that the drug in question is safe, effective and of good quality, and in every way suitable to be admitted to the national market.

The onus of proof is on the manufacturer. He will have to provide detailed evidence, drawn from trials on animals and on humans, and supported by analytical data, to show that his product satisfies these basic criteria. Usually, he also has to give a good deal of information about the process of manufacture and conversion into dosage forms. The printed packaging and attached informational leaflets must also be approved. A good deal of discretion is normally given to the licensing body, and much may turn on the exact interpretation of the regulations.

Reference to the documentation filed by the originator of a product by competitors wishing to register the same substance (e.g. as a generic), is a practice which is meeting with increasing approval by some licensing authorities, who consider that this will promote the availability of a cheaper alternative to the original product and also avoid the repetition of tests on laboratory animals. However, the fact that the second applicant may refer to the material filed, without the permission of the original manufacturer and without payment of compensation for the use of data compiled at considerable cost, has aroused the concern of research-based firms.

In a number of Member countries, once new drug approval for safety and efficacy has been obtained, a second phase of the registration processes then takes place, during which the issues discussed concern the price at which the new product is to be marketed, and its registration on the list of the drugs benefiting from government supported, or regulated third-party payments. This second aspect of registration is discussed again below.

From the standpoint of trade related issues, national registration procedures for the admission and marketing of drugs represent a form of regulatory non-tariff barriers which may affect trade in two ways, through

- differences in the standards applied by the regulatory bodies of different countries, or

- differences in the treatment given by countries to indigenous and imported drugs.

With regard to the first aspect, it is not apparent initially that important differences exist between Member countries. In practice however, the situation is more complicated. A great deal depends on the general approach of the regulatory body. A key area of uncertainty is clinical and toxicological testing. Most countries are willing to consider information of this kind obtained elsewhere, but, of course, it does not necessarily follow that they will accept it. On the whole, trials carried out in Northern Europe and North America command greater confidence than those undertaken elsewhere. It is also significant that the USA (followed in this respect by Canada) requires the submission of unusually long and detailed protocols, so much so that, in view of the importance of the American market, many large companies now test to US standards.

A number of studies have suggested that the severity of United States regulatory bodies has been a strong factor in encouraging US firms to set up R&D and manufacturing facilities in major markets where new drug approval is quicker to obtain. The level and pattern of US trade in pharmaceuticals also appear to have strongly been affected by the legislation which forbids export of drugs until they have received FDA approval, even in instances where they obtain the approval of the authorities of the country to which the exports are intended. A recent US report has qualified this anomaly as the single most important barrier to US exports (13) and recommendations have been made as to the way it might be partly resolved (14).

The extent to which the process of new drug approval stricto sensu (as opposed to the fixing of prices) is used to discriminate between imported and locally developed products is difficult to assess. In a number of Member countries, it appears to be considerably quicker and easier to obtain registration of a new drug if the clinical trials and the later stages of manufacture are carried out there. Japan requires all clinical tests to be carried out on native Japanese since dosage and drug tolerance of Japanese are different from those of inhabitants of other countries (15). However, the profession considers that there are a number of other countries (16) where the approach taken by regulatory bodies either at the new drug approval stage or at that of registration and pricing or at both, makes domestic manufacturing from local plant the safest way of marketing. The choice between investment and exports is one, of course, which is not open to all firms: here as in other instances small firms are at a disadvantage.

The area of new drug approval is one where international harmonisation of standards and procedures between countries which possess, as in the case of OECD, very similar aims and criteria appears in principle as being both desirable and feasable. Such harmonisation would obviously reduce the effect of regulatory barriers to trade. In this regard consideration should be given to the decision of the OECD Council of May 12, 1981 in a somewhat similar area. This decision concerns the mutual acceptance of data in the assessment of chemicals. The Council agreed "that data generated in the testing of chemicals in OECD Member countries in accordance with OECD test guidelines and OECD principles of good laboratory practice shall be accepted in other member countries for purposes of assessment and other uses relating to protection of man and environment".

National procedures for approval of drugs have been progressively harmonized in the EEC over the last 20 years. Several EEC directives, which are legally binding, regulate the conditions and time limits for drug approval, the requirements for analytical, pharmo-toxicological and clinical testing, the conditions for manufacture and control of drugs, and labelling requirements. Firms may approach each member State separately for drug approval, or use of a multistate application procedure through the Committee for Proprietary Medicinal Products. 37 applications have followed this second procedure since 1980.

Under EEC pharmaceutical legislation, drugs manufactured and controlled in one member State can be imported in another member State without being re-controlled. Testing data are mutually accepted without repetition since 1977. Once the process of applying the Community requirements to old drugs on the market has been completed, which may be expected to take place by 1990 at the latest, the establishment of a real common market for drugs through the mutual recognition of national drug approvals should become possible.

The effective existence of a common market for drugs within the EEC would permit some economies of scale in manufacturing which the segmented European markets now render difficult. This might favour mainly large companies and would certainly lead to a reorganisation of the industry in EEC countries. The present system, however, with its premium in favour of multinational investment, is also one which places the small firm at a disadvantage.

2. Controls over prices

In almost all Member countries the government is heavily involved in the health care system, spending on which often makes up a substantial and generally rising proportion of the national budget. During the two decades following the Second World War, the very strong expansion of third-party payments for health-care costs played a major part in the expansion of the pharmaceutical industry and the prosperity of firms.

Today the situation has changed. In a number of countries generic products have gained considerable favour with the public and with hospitals and some practitioners in reaction to the excessive proliferation of "me-too" products resulting from spurious "new-product" competition and agressive advertising of proprietary OTC drugs. National administrations have been forced at the same time to look for economies in health care expenditure. Although spending on drugs is typically only 5-15 per cent of the health care total, it is usually easier to control in political terms than other items of health expenditures. Legal proceedings taken against some major pharmaceutical companies for alleged monopolistic pricing and abuse of dominant market positions have also served to justify price controls.

Most governments today try therefore to control pharmaceutical expenditure either by regulating the prices of individual prescription drugs, by limiting total spending, or by encouraging competition from cheap sources, notably the production and use of generics (17).

The methods used to regulate the prices of prescription drugs vary from country to country within OECD. Only in the USA and Canada is the cost charged in full to most patients (18). In all other nations the State meets part of the bill. By far the most common system is one in which the patient pays a flat sum to the pharmacist who dispenses the drug and is himself reimbursed by a state or semi-state agency for the difference between the standard charge and the actual selling price of the product. In other countries, the patient pays in full and is later reimbursed by the state or semi-state agency.

Most -- but not all -- governments list the drugs which qualify for reimbursement and the extent to which they do so. The majority -- again, there are exceptions -- also control the price at which a product may be introduced and the degree to which that price may subsequently be increased. In most Member countries the price is normally fixed by reference to the therapeutic value of the drug, its cost of production, and the price of similar products. With imported drugs, the selling price in the country of origin is often taken into account.

In some countries an allowance for the research element it incorporates may be made. This is usually reserved to firms which do R&D domestically and has been used as an incentive to foreign companies to set up R&D facilities. This is strictly speaking an instrument of industrial policy.

The United Kingdom follows a different strategy from most other countries. No attempt is made to control the prices of individual drugs. Instead, annual agreements are made with each company about the total sum to be paid by the National Health Service for its products. The sum in question is designed to assure the firm of a reasonable rate of return on its capital, taking into account here again its UK research effort and other overheads.

The USA and Canada have taken a different path again. There is no general control of drug prices, but many individual states and provinces authorise the substitution of cheap generic products for branded drugs, and encourage the use of generics in other ways.

Pricing policies can create trade-related issues in two ways:

- the distortions in the pattern of trade to which the absence of any real "world market price" for drug may lead; and

- the possibility which is opened for discrimination between domestic and foreign manufacturers.

Pricing policies undoubtedly have effects on the structure of trade. Since each country is effectively its own master, drug prices vary considerably (19). These price differences have created problems in Europe in particular, where they give rise to the phenomenon of parallel importing. In such a system branded drugs from one country are bought in a second where they are cheap and shipped to a third where they are more expensive (20). This practice has become endemic over the past decade. Although accounting for only a small proportion of the trade in finished drugs, parallel importing makes it difficult for companies to maintain a coherent price structure. National authorities in some Member countries have recently considered that parallel importing may also be a source of differential trading profits for importing pharmacists and have sought to deal with this issue. This de facto recognition of the dual import structure may be seen as a further expression of the increasing irrationality of the pricing system.

In principle, of course, countries with low prices should be unattractive export markets compared to those where they are high. It is possible that this plays some part in keeping down the level of pharmaceutical exports to Southern Europe. But it is extremely difficult to appreciate the impact of this factor vis-à-vis the other factors influencing the level and structure of trade, notably foreign direct investment.

Pricing policies may also include discriminatory pricing by national health authorities of imported drugs. One approach is to restrict the price of the imported drug to the wholesale price in the country of origin. Another approach is to fix the level in relation to the lowest price in the world market or in a regional market.

The use of pricing policies to control imports is insidious and difficult to detect. As the European Commission has remarked, "the fixing of prices that are too low or the debarring of a medicine from reimbursement constitute a barrier just as effective as the refusal of marketing authorisation" (21).

The extent of such behaviour is difficult to assess. Delays in the admission of new drugs to the reimbursement list have been reported from many European countries, but examples of the discriminatory use of the process appear to be comparatively rare. As noted above it is not uncommon however for better prices to be allowed to companies that carry out research in a country or commit themselves to export part of their local production. Such incentives are usually offered to both domestic and foreign firms. They tend to favour the former rather than the latter, and are an incentive to set up plant domestically. They are best seen as a measure used to strengthen local industrial capacity rather than as a barrier to imports.

3.   Government policies for the development of the domestic industry

Government may act in a variety of ways to assist the development of the domestic industry. When considering their policies, it is necessary to differentiate between those which aim at increasing the national capacity for production and that for innovation. The former is to a considerable extent within the grasp of many countries, but the latter needs far more resources, in the form of finance but more particularly in that of scarce human resources and rare industrial skills.

Policies seeking to increase the national capacity for production may themselves have a range of objectives: developing an export orientated industry mainly aimed at sales to foreign markets; developing a capacity for cheap drug production with a priority notably for generic products; building up the basis for an industry which in time is expected to develop a capacity for innovation.

While the mix of policy instruments will differ in each instance, the range of instruments open to governments is fairly limited. It includes pricing policies, tax and other investment incentives which can be aimed at production or innovation objectives and at foreign or domestic firms according to the priorities chosen, public purchasing policies, patent policies, and measures for fostering industrial reorganisation and mergers.

a) Investment and export promotion incentives and requirements addressed to foreign firms

In the Third World many governments have sought to build up a local capacity for drug production and have taken steps to do so. Most frequently this has been confined to the conversion of bulk drugs to dosage forms, but some have begun the manufacture of active ingredients. One set of policies adopted by a number of countries following the objective has been to offer important incentives to foreign firms.

In OECD countries industrial policy in pharmaceuticals is more often aimed at upgrading indigenous capacities through R&D and developing exports. In a number of countries incentives have been offered to foreign firms for fostering these objectives. Product approval and pricing policies may also be used to ensure the cooperation of firms. In some OECD countries, firms may find that applications for product approval, import licences, and other requirements are more promptly reviewed if exports, local manufacture, or local research and development are increased. They may find likewise that price increases will not be granted unless they agree to help in meeting export objectives.

Ireland has evolved an original and extensive foreign investment incentives policy aimed in particular at the promotion of exports and the creation of jobs. As part of a policy of attracting modern industry, new companies have been exempted from income and profits tax on their export earnings for 15 years. Generous tax allowances and grants for capital investment are also available. These concessions have produced a rapidly growing pharmaceutical sector, totally export-oriented and concentrating on the production of active ingredients. The firms involved are almost all affiliates of foreign multinationals.

b) Public purchasing policies

A further instrument for strengthening a local industry is to discriminate in its favour in purchases for the public sector. This is almost impossible in the high-technology sector, where buyers have to deal with the suppliers of products under patent protection or decide to forego their use, which is of course quite exceptional within OECD. In the generic drug field, however, the existence of multiple sources makes discrimination in favour of local manufacturers or of lowest bidders possible.

The strategy of reserving this segment of the market for local manufacturers is common in the developing countries, where it has been advocated by the WHO and UNCTAD. Within OECD it is generally confined to Member countries where the pharmaceutical industry is at a relatively early stage of development. In Greece, hospitals are obliged to use Greek drugs unless none are available, and Portugal has a policy of giving preference to local producers in buying multi-source drugs for the State health-care system.

c) Policies in the area of patents

Patent policy can be used as an instrument for building up a domestic capacity for production. It permits the initial development of an industry which is based at the start on the copy of foreign drugs. Prior to its revision in 1975 the Japanese patent law offered protection only to "processes", but not to "substances". It did not recognise product patents. Firms could produce imitations of drugs sold by other firms so long as a different process for production could be found. In Italy, Article 14 of the Patent Law denied all protection to pharmaceutical products or processes. A ruling by the Constitution Court of 20th March 1978 declared this Article to be unconstitutional. Consequently, since that ruling pharmaceutical products and processes are subject to patenting in the same conditions as any other chemical product. In Europe, Austria, Portugal and Yugoslavia still only protect processes, and Spain also gives only a limited form of protection to products.

In Europe the European Patent Convention agreed in 1972 has established a single European patent system. Under the European Convention both pharmaceutical products and the processes by which they are made are protected for a period of 20 years from the time of registration. Only a single patent is required to give protection to firms in all participating countries, which include most European countries of high and medium capacity.

Canada has followed its own path in this area. Patent protection is limited and the compulsory licensing of products to local firms encouraged. This has contributed to the decision of several multinationals to run down their Canadian research activities. Canadian aims differ from those of most other Member countries in that they are not aimed at the emergence of an innovative local industry and have made the supply of cheap drugs their central objective. In this, Canada resembles a number of countries outside OECD, who consider that they have little prospect of creating a research-based industry in the near future, and that their immediate interest lies in acquiring a reasonable range of products at the lowest possible cost. Reasonable as this aim may be, it is not without disadvantages. Innovative companies are reluctant to invest in nations which do not offer adequate patent protection, and cannot but take a cautious attitude towards developing products whose main markets would lie there.

Firms generally view compulsory licensing and renewable patents as restraints on their freedom of decision and as a weakening of the protection of their industrial property rights. Legislation imposing compulsory licences when patents have not been sufficiently worked has been adopted by some Member countries, notably Canada, Greece and Yugoslavia. In this system licences may also be imposed if the patent owner refuses to license his patent or imposes "unjustified conditions" or "unreasonable terms" on the licensee. In Greece, the grantee of the compulsory licence may proceed immediately with the exploitation of the invention, before the compensation payable to the patent owner has been determined by a court of law. Greek law has also established a system of renewable patents. The first patent lasts for seven years and is renewed if certain conditions are met, such as "sufficiently working" the patent, or meeting "the reasonable requirements of the public".

Weak patent protection may, in some instances, also influence the level and structure of trade by forcing foreign producers to select a local firm as a co-marketer of a new product as the only sure way of ensuring that local competitors do not copy the product. The local firm handles the procedures with the registration authorities, who then approve the drug for sale by the local and foreign producer jointly. In exchange the registration authorities agree to prevent marketing or copying of the new drug by any other local company.

Patent protection is considered by the profession as being vital to the well-being of the high-technology part of the pharmaceutical industry. The extremely high costs of innovation mean that under present circumstances, a qualified monopoly of ownership is absolutely necessary if the innovator is to recover his costs and maintain research for the future. One of the major reasons for introduction of full patent protection by Japan in 1975 derived from a recognition of the fact that the level of development reached by their firms at that time required that this monopoly be granted so as to permit them to launch into R&D and innovation in a major way.

In the United States the "restoration of effective patent time" which was considered by US firms to be considerably reduced by lengthy FDA regulatory procedures (22) has been materialised recently by the 1984 Waxman-Hatch Act which extended the patent lifetime by up to five years in exchange for concessions on the provision of safety and other data by the discoverers of a drug to those who wished to market it as a generic once the patent expired. It is too early to assess whether this will modify the strategies and competitiveness of US firms. A similar move is contemplated in Europe.

An important recent development in the United States has been the decision taken in 1980 to permit universities to retain patent rights on all inventions arising from federally supported research (23). The implications of the decision have been discussed principally from the standpoint of traditional academic values. It is too early to assess their possible effect on the international diffusion of the results of US government funded R&D in health.

d) Industrial restructuring and government supported mergers

During the past decade several larger developed nations have taken active steps to strengthen the innovative capacity of their industries. These have usually included the encouragement of research, most commonly by tax concessions and pricing policies of the type discussed above. In some countries policies have been adopted with the aim of ensuring the restructuring of the industry and the creation of larger and therefore more viable units. France is a case in point. For many years a certain lack of satisfaction by government with the organisation of the French pharmaceutical industry has been apparent. The measures taken had resulted by 1980 in the emergence of two large domestically controlled industrial groups from a previously fragmented industry. One is owned by private capital only, the second jointly by public and private capital. A new phase of industrial restructuring following the nationalisation of some major industrial groups may take this process further. Italy has intermittently followed such policies, and Spain has also recently announced a programme of industrial restructuring.

4. Trade related issues and the innovative capacities of firms

Mention has been made repeatedly of the effects which a number of government policies -- along with the business practices followed by large firms as a normal part of their strategies (notably in the granting of licensing) -- may have had on the viability of small and medium innovative pharmaceutical companies. The rising cost of R&D and innovation represent a major factor in the increasing concentration of the industry, while many government policies offer de facto a premium to firms who are in a position to adopt the multinational form of operation.

Consequently innovative capacities in pharmaceuticals are now lodged, to a very large extent, essentially within the largest multinational enterprises. Although they have been able to meet the rising cost of R&D and innovation through their multinational form of operation, and have benefited from the overall process of concentration of innovative capacity, these firms may also be affected in their turn by the measures which have just been discussed.

As has been seen above, innovation in the pharmaceutical industry is characterised by heavy expenditure and long lead times. Many products survive the rigorous development process to reach the market and then fail. The risks involved are considerable. The innovative companies need therefore to maintain a high cash flow. Policies which reduce their ability to do so are to their disadvantage. Almost all the measures and policies in this section fall into this category. Delays in approving new drugs, price controls and restrictions on the import of finished drugs obviously limit the extent to which companies are able to realise the full commercial potential of their product range. Controls over imports can be and are circumvented by adopting multinational forms of organisation, but this policy has its drawbacks. In particular, economies of scale in production are more difficult to obtain.

Policies intended to strengthen local pharmaceutical industries may also work against the interests of the innovative world-scale firm. Discrimination in favour of domestic producers in public-sector purchasing, subsidies to local companies and limitation of patent protection cannot but reduce the cash flow of such firms. Moreover, although this report has concentrated on high-technology pharmaceutical products, it should always be remembered that the innovative companies continue to market and to depend for their cash flow on drugs which they have developed or licensed and which are now out-of-patent. Their sales of generics under brand names often make a considerable contribution to total profits. Thus, measures to encourage the use of locally made commodity generics can also adversely affect the innovative capacity of the large firm.

On the other grounds, notably of cheapness and social equity, measures such as those favouring the promotion of generic products will, on the contrary, be seen by many governments and large segments of public opinion as important and highly legitimate. There is no easy and certainly no single reply to the problem posed by the existence of contradictory situations of this nature. They are an expression of the complexity encountered by many social issues at the stage now reached in the economic and social development of Member countries, and require consequently a careful and balanced consideration.

NOTES AND REFERENCES

1. See the study prepared for the CSTP during the activity on multinational enterprises and national scientific and technical capacity, M.L. Burstall, J.H. Dunning and A. Lake: Multinational Enterprises, Governments and Technology - The Pharmaceutical Industry, OECD, Paris, 1981. The study is available as a background document to this report.

2. For a discussion of the problems involved in measuring economic activity in the pharmaceutical industry, see Annex. The category "intermediates" includes all products other than drugs in dosage forms which are made or used by the industry.

3. According to the Dutch pharmaceutical manufacturers' association NEFARMA, the number of individual products on sale was 15 000 in the UK and Germany, 13 700 in Italy, 8 000 in Belgium and France, and 3 566 in the Netherlands (Scrip, 14/10/81, 634, 4).

4. A recent survey showed that OTC drugs were 17 per cent of Western European consumption in 1979. They made up 11 per cent of the total in Austria, 10 per cent in Belgium, 12 per cent in France, 18 per cent in Germany, 5 per cent in Italy, 12 per cent in the Netherlands, 11 per cent in Spain, 10 per cent in Sweden, 35 per cent in Switzerland, and 21 per cent in the UK. (Scrip, 31/8/81, 621, 4). In the United States, OTC drugs represent 13 per cent of the market.

5. There is a good deal of overlap between the generic and OTC categories. Countries vary a good deal in what they allow to be sold without prescription, and a drug which is an OTC product in one country may be a generic in another. Moreover, OTC drugs are often obtained by prescription, especially where this is to the advantage of the patient. Thus it is difficult to estimate with any precision the overall market shares of such drugs.

6. See Factbook, 1980 edition, of the Pharmaceutical Manufacturers' Association of America.

7. It is fairly easy to determine the extent of trade in finished drugs, but much more difficult to do so for intermediates. For this reason, the figures quoted for intermediates are therefore only indicative.

8. A very relevant recent calculation is by J. Thesing: Industrielle Arzneimittelforschung Heute, Mainz, 1983: Medizinisch Pharmazeutische Studiengesellschaft eV., which claims that for each NEC marketed by German firms in the decade 1972-1981 the cost was $60 million. This includes the costs of developing products that never reached the market.

9. Some new developments have taken place in the United States in the patenting of government funded R&D.

10. A.T. Bull, G. Holt and M.D. Lilly, Biotechnology: International Trends and Perspectives, OECD, Paris, (to be published).

11. See Burstall, Dunning and Lake, op. cit., pp. 181-182.

12. OTA, Impact of Applied Genetics: Micro-organisms, Plants and Animals, Congress of the United States, Washington, D.C., 1981, p. 55.

13. US Department of Commerce, An Assessment of US Competitiveness in High Technology Industries, Washington, D.C., February 1983, p. 63.

14. National Research Council, The Competitive Status of the US Pharmaceutical Industry, Washington, D.C., 1983, Chapter 5.

15. The Japanese Health Authorities are now willing to consider information obtained from tests on Japanese living outside Japan.

16. Notably those where the import penetration of finished products as opposed to intermediates, is low, or lower, at least, than their level of domestic innovative capacity would lead to expect [see Annex, Table A7].

17. The prices of OTC drugs are controlled much less severely since they are not generally reimbursed to patients. In many countries they are not controlled at all.

18. Under the Medicaid scheme for the elderly, drugs are subsidised, but of course, this covers only a minority of the population.

19. See W.D. Reekie : Price Comparisons of Identical Products in Japan, the United States and Europe, Office of Health Economics, London, 1981. For the European situation see the figures given by the Italian manufacturers' association quoted in Scrip, 1981, 608, 6.

20. For general accounts of parallel importing, see IMS Pharmaceutical Monitor, November 1982, pp. 27-28 and Scrip, 8/6/81, 570, 2.

21. European Commission: Report on Pharmaceutical Preparations [Com. (80) 789 (Final)], Brussels, 1981.

22. See The Competitive Status of the US Pharmaceutical Industry, op. cit., Chapter 5.

23. The decisions were taken as a result of the Uniform Federal Patent Policy Act.

COMPLEMENTARY STATISTICAL TABLES

A note on methodological difficulties

There are real difficulties in measuring production, consumption and trade in the pharmaceutical industry. Because of the multiplicity of products they must be expressed in monetary terms, by convention US dollars. In times of inflation and changing exchange rates this presents obvious problems.

The data available is often only approximate. Statistics of consumption refer normally to human pharmaceuticals but may include veterinary products. They may or may not include generic products. In this report they are taken from Scrip and from IMS Pharmaceutical Newsletter and probably come ultimately from the market research firm Intercontinental Medical Statistics. They are probably fairly accurate. Production statistics are less so. They may or may not include intermediates which are later converted into finished products ready for administration. They are taken mainly from the OECD publication: The Chemical Industry, 1980 edition, Paris, 1982, and from national sources.

Trade statistics are gathered on a uniform basis internationally, notably by the United Nations and by OECD. They differentiate between medicinal, etc. products (SITC 541) and various sub-categories, of which medicaments (SITC 5417) is the most important. This latter includes all products made up for retail sale together with bulk mixtures requiring conversion into pills, etc. In this report category 5417 is referred to as "finished drugs". Intermediates are more difficult to estimate. SITC categories 5413 to 5416 comprise a number of important active materials but many others are hidden in completely different parts of the standard classification. In this report intermediates are taken to be the difference between goods in category 541 and those in 5417. The reader is warned that this underestimates considerably the trade in intermediates. It does, however, appear to lead to the correct qualitative conclusions.

The classification of countries

Developed countries are OECD Member countries plus Israel, and South Africa.

The Eastern bloc is CMEA plus the People's Republic of China.

List of Tables

List of Figures

Table Al

WORLD CONSUMPTION OF PHARMACEUTICALS IN 1980

Country	Consumption ($ Million)	Population (Million)	GDP ($Bill.)	Consumption		
				Per Capita	As % GDP	As % Health Care Spending
Austria	430	7.51	77.0	57	0.56	12
Belgium	780	9.86	119.3	79	0.65	
Denmark	215	5.12	66.4	42	0.32	
Finland	240	4.78	53.7	50	0.48	12
France	4 950	53.71	652.7	92	0.76	10
Germany	5 050	61.56	814.8	81	0.62	6
Greece	440	9.64	40.1	46	1.10	
Ireland	130	3.40	18.0	38	0.72	10
Italy	3 200	57.04	395.9	56	0.83	13
Netherlands	580	14.14	168.9	41	0.34	5
Norway	160	4.07	57.4	39	0.28	5
Portugal	350	9.88	24.1	36	1.45	
Spain	1 950	37.43	210.4	52	0.93	22
Sweden	530	8.31	123.4	63	0.44	6
Switzerland	580	6.37	101.6	91	0.57	8
United Kingdom	2 150	55.95	526.0	38	0.41	10
USA	12 610	227.66	2,587.0	55	0.49	5
Canada	950	23.94	256.5	40	0.37	
Australia	530	14.62	139.7	36	0.38	
Japan	13 150	116.78	1 040.4	113	1.26	
Other developed	750					
CMEA	11 000					
Developed countries	11 500					
Total	72 000					

Note : At manufacturers' prices and contemporary US dollars at the exchange rates then prevailing. Compiled from Scrip, various issues, 1981-1982.

Table A2

WORLD PRODUCTION OF PHARMACEUTICALS IN 1980

Country	Production ($ Million)	Production as % Chemical Output
Austria	390	7
Belgium	850	9
Denmark	450	23
Finland	196	7
France	5 950	16
Germany	8 405	14
Greece	370	
Ireland	175	
Italy	3 950	
Netherlands	775	5
Norway	80	4
Portugal	300	
Spain	2 350	13
Sweden	570	12
Switzerland	2 400	
United Kingdom	4 150	10
United States	16 150	10
Canada	1 150	
Australia	620	11
Japan	15 500	
Other developed	500	
CMEA	11 000	
Developing countries	9 500	
Total	85 000	

Note : At manufacturers' prices and contemporary US dollars. Compiled from
Scrip, various issues, 1981-1982; IMS Pharmaceutical Newsletter,
various issues, 1981-1983; The Chemical Industry 1980, OECD, Paris,
1982; World Development, 1983, 11, (3) (Special issue on the
pharmaceutical industry in the developing countries).

World consumption is human-use drugs sold to final consumers,
expressed in manufacturers' prices. World production may include
veterinary products and intermediates which are later turned into
dosage forms. Accordingly, production figures always exceed
consumption figures.

Table A3

TOTAL IMPORTS OF PHARMACEUTICAL PRODUCTS 1960-1980
WITH BREAKDOWN BY FINISHED DRUGS AND INTERMEDIATES FOR 1980
(excluding CMEA and China)

| Country | Total Imports ($Million) | | | | 1980 | |
	1960	1970	1980	As % all Imports	Finished Drugs ($Million)	Intermediates ($Million)
Austria	12	51	350	1.43	240	110
Belgium	45	138	655	0.92	446	209
Denmark	14	45	206	1.06	125	81
Finland	11	34	134	0.86	96	38
France	8	144	701	0.52	141	560
Germany	35	175	1 291	0.69	751	540
Greece			161	1.53	98	63
Ireland		29	156	1.40	121	35
Italy	37	143	652	0.66	252	400
Netherlands	19	111	568	0.74	411	157
Norway	7	26	138	0.81	107	31
Portugal	11	37	170	1.81	107	63
Spain	6	63	274	0.72	54	220
Sweden	19	72	326	0.97	263	63
Switzerland	18	78	411	1.13	227	184
United Kingdom	15	81	517	0.43	322	195
USA	26	87	803	0.31	309	494
Canada	25	80	356	0.61	109	247
Australia	36	68	180	0.84	93	87
Japan	17	216	1 074	0.76	530	544
Developing countries	450	1 020	4 450		2 750	1 700

Sources: Trade by Commodities, OECD; Commodity Trade Statistics, United Nations.

50

Table A4

TOTAL EXPORTS OF PHARMACEUTICAL PRODUCTS 1960-1980
(excluding CMEA and China)

Country	Total Exports ($Million)			As % all Imports	Finished Drugs ($Million)	Intermediates ($Million)
	1960	1970	1980			
Austria	3	14	201	1.15	119	82
Belgium	17	83	669	1.04	547	122
Denmark	23	61	308	1.87	237	71
Finland		2	50	0.35	24	26
France	80	230	1 497	1.35	1 149	348
Germany	115	491	2 272	1.18	1 379	893
Greece			22		16	6
Ireland		23	165	1.94	68	97
Italy	37	154	686	0.88	306	380
Netherlands	44	141	595	0.81	387	208
Norway	1	5	36	0.19	12	24
Portugal	3	14	44	0.99	21	23
Spain	1	12	191	0.92	83	108
Sweden	17	35	315	0.99	248	57
Switzerland	117	329	1 615	5.45	1 021	594
United Kingdom	136	335	1 734	1.56	1 217	517
USA	275	422	2 036	0.94	711	1 325
Canada		25	112	0.18	52	62
Australia	5	23	95	0.43	49	46
Japan	17	66	294	0.23	62	232
Developing countries		170	500		150	350
World	950	2 800	14 000			

Note : See Table A3.

Table A5

EXPORTS OF FINISHED DRUGS 1980 IN $ Million
(excluding CMEA and China)

To \ From	Austria	Belgium	Denmark	France	Germany	Italy	Netherlands	Spain	Sweden	Switzerland	United Kingdom	Other Europe	United States	Canada	Australia	Japan	Other developed	Developing	World
Austria		11	8	9	123	6	11		10	31	14	2	2					5	227
Belgium	3		7	84	116	18	66	4	5	55	35	1	26	5					430
Denmark	3	9		7	18	4	12	2	16	14	22	4	2						117
Finland		7	15	1	13		9		14	13	13	1	3						89
France	47	24	2		20	8	25		11	15	30	1	6						143
Germany	2	113	19	132		44	53	6	37	132	87	10	27			5			718
Greece		4	3	7	19	2	8			34	10		3	1		1		2	92
Ireland		2	2	1	5		2		1	4	98		5	2					120
Italy	16	24	7	27	101		19	2	18	49	20		10	1				2	278
Netherlands	2	136	17	46	69			2	37	29	35	9	44	1					420
Norway		6	14	2	16	1	12		1	12	12	9							93
Portugal	3	6	3	3	4	2	6	4	3	42	18		2						101
Spain	1	4	4	9	58	6	4			2	6								57
Sweden	8	21	33	42	88	10	23	1		31	52	8	20						248
Switzerland	6	22	7	31	83	8	13	5	4		22	1	5	2	2				245
United Kingdom		16	24		49		22	2	23	39		23	49					4	334
USA	1	1	4	1	7	40	4		5	5	11	1		8		20		50	157
Canada		4		3	4	2	1		4	4	17	1	64						103
Australia			4						10	7	30	2	18				1		92
Japan	3	2	8	33	138		11	14	6	94	29	3	89					17	436
Developing																			
Africa	2	37	14	552	107	52	21	13		75	190	22	18						1 105
Dev. America	4	8	4	41	70	7	8	17		47	47	2	137	2					392
Dev. Asia	4	20	5	34	102	25	10			90	79		73						437
Middle East																			
OPEC	5	42	30	45	110	39	13	14		139	176	1	28	1					643
World	114	526	236	1 126	1 333	283	343	72	207	1 003	1 112	116	670	28	33	26	2	82	7 500

Note : From the export tables of SITC 5417, 1980; OECD: Trade by Commodities. Certain categories are omitted, so that the individual rows and columns do not total.

EXPORTS OF INTERMEDIATES 1980 IN $ Million
(excluding CMEA and China)

To \ From	Austria	Belgium	Denmark	France	Germany	Italy	Netherlands	Spain	Sweden	Switzerland	United Kingdom	Other Europe	United States	Japan	Other developed	Developing	World
Austria	1	3	1	3	41	2	2		1	14	5		31			3	106
Belgium	3			26	24	4	9	1	4	15	24	32	116	3		22	278
Denmark		3		3	30		1		14	6	8	1	1	1		4	86
Finland	1	1	2	1	4	4	1		8	1	2		1			1	33
France	12	32	15		82	66	25	5	2	84	36	4	155	13	7	15	563
Germany	22	13	5	43		34	57	21	3	96	52		107	2	6	50	535
Greece	1	15	3	3	9	11	1			7	4		7				57
Ireland				2	4					1	17		12			2	42
Italy	3	4	3	22	97		16	5	5	65	46		72	4	2	12	358
Netherlands		8	1	18	36	16		7	2	6	43		23	6		14	175
Norway		5	3	1	12		2		9	3	3	2	1				41
Portugal		2		10	9	5	2	2		13	10	13	1			1	53
Spain		8	4	17	34	21			1	36	17	2	30	4	5	10	184
Sweden		2	2	3	15		2	1		6	7	1			1	2	64
Switzerland	6	4	1	24	58	58	4	5	1		18		73	6	3	9	242
United Kingdom	1	6	4	10	23	6	10	1	1			3		2	1	7	175
USA	3	2	6	15	95	28	8	4	14	42	37	27		52	12	7	404
Canada			1	3	10	6	1		1	13	15		86	5			140
Australia		2	1	2	10					3	10	2	21		2		53
Japan		2	2	15	43	28	7	20	7	25	24		241		9	123	540
Developing																	
Africa	7	5	3	67	40	9	4	2	5	21	88	9	9	4			275
Dev. America	6	4	9	29	104	30	14	15	12	61	36		191	15	36		555
Dev. Asia	4	8		16	54	61	9	10		24	60		67	40	10		375
Middle East			6	5		2	2	4	8	22	20			4			
OPEC	4	3			32		2						12				129
World	79	137	80	356	910	398	184	116	101	592	595	123	1 335	161	116	123	6 000

Note : For source see Methodological Note. Certain categories are omitted, so that the individual rows and columns do not total.

Table A7

IMPORT PENETRATION AND NATIONAL CAPACITY, 1980

Country	National Capacity	Imports of Finished Drugs as % consumption	% Imports from					
			High Capacity Countries		Medium Capacity Countries		Low Capacity Countries	
			Finished	Intermediates	Finished	Intermediates	Finished	Intermediates
Austria	Low	56	77	89	20	7	2	4
Belgium	Medium	57	74	74	23	11	3	15
Denmark	Medium	58	53	56	36	21	11	23
Finland	Low	40	48	27	47	48	5	25
France	High	3	40	65	50	27	10	8
Germany	High	15	53	56	44	10	3	34
Greece	Low	23	79	51	21	47		2
Ireland	Low	95	95	88	4	7	1	5
Italy	Medium	8	74	84	24	8	2	8
Netherlands	Medium	71	53	72	41	15	6	13
Norway	Low	76	26	54	55	45	19	5
Portugal	Low	31	77	81	11	13	12	6
Spain	Low	3	61	73	35	19	4	8
Sweden	Medium	51	63	60	34	10	3	30
Switzerland	High	39	71	59	21	28	8	13
United Kingdom	High	16	60	61	30	15	10	14
United States	High	2	15	54	45	31	40	15
Canada	Low	10	89	91	11	9	0	
Australia	Low	15	73	87	20	9	7	4
Japan	High	4	88	64	7	7	5	29
Other developed	Low		73		5		22	
Developing countries	Low	25	84	72	13	21	3	7

THE 25 LARGEST PHARMACEUTICAL COMPANIES IN THE WORLD, 1982

1982 Rank	1978 Rank	Name	Pharmaceutical Sales $Million	As % Total Sales	As % World Sales (1)	R&D Expenditure $Million	As % Drug Sales	Nationality
1	2	Bayer	2 452	17	3.6	300	13.5	German
2	3	Merck and Co.	2 217	72	3.3	130	6.0	American
3	6	American Home Products	2 144	47	3.1			American
4	1	Hoechst	2 071 (2)	15	3.0	219	10.6	German
5	5	Ciba-Geigy	2 054	30	3.0			Swiss
6	8	Pfizer	1 694	49	2.5	175	10.3	American
7	9	Eli Lilly	1 532	52	2.2			American
8	3	Hoffman-Laroche	1 512	42	2.2	300	19.8	Swiss
9	7	Sandoz	1 419	47	2.1	180	12.7	Swiss
10	15	Bristol-Meyers	1 360	38	2.0	140	10.2	American
11	19	Smithkline Beckmann	1 339	45	2.0	166	12.4	American
12	18	Abbott	1 300	50	1.9	120	9.2	American
13	10	Takeda	1 291	59	1.9			Japanese
14	12	Warner Lambert	1 286	40	1.9	116	9.0	American
15	11	Boehringer Ingelheim	1 214	82	1.8	185	15.2	German
16	14	Upjohn	1 213	66	1.8	160	14.3	American
17	24	Johnson & Johnson	1 119	19	1.6	90	9.1	American
18	20	Glaxo	999	83	1.4	110	11.2	British
19	16	Squibb	978	59	1.4	125	14.0	American
20	13	Rhône-Poulenc	896	16	1.3			French
21	(..)	American Cyanamid	884	26	1.3	100	11.3	American
22	17	Schering-Plough	882	49	1.3	98	11.3	American
23	25	ICI	839	7	1.2	117	14.1	British
24	(..)	Wellcome	837	80	1.2	90	11.5	British
25	23	Beecham	782	31	1.1			British

(1) Excluding CMEA.
(2) Excluding Roussel-Uclaf.
(..) Not ranked in the first 25 in 1978.

Figures from company reports and from information from Interpharma SA; Scrip, various issues; European Chemical News, various issues. R&D expenditures are approximate and should be used with caution. They have however been considered as realistic estimates by industrial experts consulted.

Figure A1

THE STRUCTURE OF EXPORTS OF FINISHED DRUGS FROM THE OECD AREA TO THE THIRD WORLD
(Base = 1 000)

From / To	France	Germany	Switzerland	UK	USA	Other Developed	Total
Developing Africa	214	42	29	74	7	63	429
Developing America	18	27	18	18	53	19	151
Developing East Asia	13	40	35	31	28	23	170
Middle Eastern OPEC	17	43	54	68	11	56	249
Total	260	152	136	191	99	161	1 000

Figure A2

THE STRUCTURE OF EXPORTS OF INTERMEDIATES FROM THE OECD AREA TO THE THIRD WORLD
(Base = 1 000)

From / To	France	Germany	Switzerland	UK	USA	Italy	Other Developed	Total
Developing Africa	50	30	16	66	7	7	30	206
Developing America	22	78	46	27	143	22	78	416
Developing East Asia	12	40	18	45	50	46	70	281
Middle Eastern OPEC	4	24	16	15	9	1	28	97
Total	88	172	96	153	209	76	206	1 000

OECD SALES AGENTS
DÉPOSITAIRES DES PUBLICATIONS DE L'OCDE

ARGENTINA – ARGENTINE
Carlos Hirsch S.R.L., Florida 165, 4° Piso (Galería Guemes)
1333 BUENOS AIRES, Tel. 33.1787.2391 y 30.7122

AUSTRALIA – AUSTRALIE
Australia and New Zealand Book Company Pty, Ltd.,
10 Aquatic Drive, Frenchs Forest, N.S.W. 2086
P.O. Box 459, BROOKVALE, N.S.W. 2100. Tel. (02) 452.44.11

AUSTRIA – AUTRICHE
OECD Publications and Information Center
4 Simrockstrasse 5300 Bonn (Germany). Tel. (0228) 21.60.45
Local Agent/Agent local :
Gerold and Co., Graben 31, WIEN 1. Tel. 52.22.35

BELGIUM – BELGIQUE
Jean De Lannoy, Service Publications OCDE
avenue du Roi 202, B-1060 BRUXELLES. Tel. 02/538.51.69

CANADA
Renouf Publishing Company Limited,
Central Distribution Centre,
61 Sparks Street (Mall),
P.O.B. 1008 - Station B,
OTTAWA, Ont. KIP 5R1.
Tel. (613)238.8985-6
Toll Free: 1-800.267.4164
Librairie Renouf Limitée
980 rue Notre-Dame,
Lachine, P.Q. H8S 2B9,
Tel. (514) 634-7088.

DENMARK – DANEMARK
Munksgaard Export and Subscription Service
35, Nørre Søgade
DK 1370 KØBENHAVN K. Tel. +45.1.12.85.70

FINLAND – FINLANDE
Akateeminen Kirjakauppa
Keskuskatu 1, 00100 HELSINKI 10. Tel. 65.11.22

FRANCE
Bureau des Publications de l'OCDE,
2 rue André-Pascal, 75775 PARIS CEDEX 16. Tel. (1) 524.81.67
Principal correspondant :
13602 AIX-EN-PROVENCE : Librairie de l'Université.
Tel. 26.18.08

GERMANY – ALLEMAGNE
OECD Publications and Information Center
4 Simrockstrasse 5300 BONN Tel. (0228) 21.60.45

GREECE – GRÈCE
Librairie Kauffmann, 28 rue du Stade,
ATHÈNES 132. Tel. 322.21.60

HONG-KONG
Government Information Services,
Publications (Sales) Office,
Beaconsfield House, 4/F.,
Queen's Road Central

ICELAND – ISLANDE
Snaebjörn Jónsson and Co., h.f.,
Hafnarstraeti 4 and 9, P.O.B. 1131, REYKJAVIK.
Tel. 13133/14281/11936

INDIA – INDE
Oxford Book and Stationery Co. :
NEW DELHI-1, Scindia House. Tel. 45896
CALCUTTA 700016, 17 Park Street. Tel. 240832

INDONESIA – INDONÉSIE
PDIN-LIPI, P.O. Box 3065/JKT., JAKARTA, Tel. 583467

IRELAND – IRLANDE
TDC Publishers – Library Suppliers
12 North Frederick Street, DUBLIN 1 Tel. 744835-749677

ITALY – ITALIE
Libreria Commissionaria Sansoni :
Via Lamarmora 45, 50121 FIRENZE. Tel. 579751/584468
Via Bartolini 29, 20155 MILANO. Tel. 365083
Sub-depositari :
Ugo Tassi
Via A. Farnese 28, 00192 ROMA. Tel. 310590
Editrice e Libreria Herder,
Piazza Montecitorio 120, 00186 ROMA. Tel. 6794628
Costantino Ercolano, Via Generale Orsini 46, 80132 NAPOLI. Tel. 405210
Libreria Hoepli, Via Hoepli 5, 20121 MILANO. Tel. 865446
Libreria Scientifica, Dott. Lucio de Biasio "Aeiou"
Via Meravigli 16, 20123 MILANO Tel. 807679
Libreria Zanichelli
Piazza Galvani 1/A, 40124 Bologna Tel. 237389
Libreria Lattes, Via Garibaldi 3, 10122 TORINO. Tel. 519274
La diffusione delle edizioni OCSE è inoltre assicurata dalle migliori librerie nelle
città più importanti.

JAPAN – JAPON
OECD Publications and Information Center,
Landic Akasaka Bldg., 2-3-4 Akasaka,
Minato-ku, TOKYO 107 Tel. 586.2016

KOREA – CORÉE
Pan Korea Book Corporation,
P.O. Box n° 101 Kwangwhamun, SÉOUL. Tel. 72.7369

LEBANON – LIBAN
Documenta Scientifica/Redico,
Edison Building, Bliss Street, P.O. Box 5641, BEIRUT.
Tel. 354429 – 344425

MALAYSIA – MALAISIE
University of Malaya Co-operative Bookshop Ltd.
P.O. Box 1127, Jalan Pantai Baru
KUALA LUMPUR. Tel. 577701/577072

THE NETHERLANDS – PAYS-BAS
Staatsuitgeverij, Verzendboekhandel,
Chr. Plantijnstraat 1 Postbus 20014
2500 EA S-GRAVENHAGE. Tel. nr. 070.789911
Voor bestellingen: Tel. 070.789208

NEW ZEALAND – NOUVELLE-ZÉLANDE
Publications Section,
Government Printing Office Bookshops:
AUCKLAND: Retail Bookshop: 25 Rutland Street,
Mail Orders: 85 Beach Road, Private Bag C.P.O.
HAMILTON: Retail: Ward Street,
Mail Orders, P.O. Box 857
WELLINGTON: Retail: Mulgrave Street (Head Office),
Cubacade World Trade Centre
Mail Orders: Private Bag
CHRISTCHURCH: Retail: 159 Hereford Street,
Mail Orders: Private Bag
DUNEDIN: Retail: Princes Street
Mail Order: P.O. Box 1104

NORWAY – NORVÈGE
J.G. TANUM A/S
P.O. Box 1177 Sentrum OSLO 1. Tel. (02) 80.12.60

PAKISTAN
Mirza Book Agency, 65 Shahrah Quaid-E-Azam, LAHORE 3.
Tel. 66839

PORTUGAL
Livraria Portugal, Rua do Carmo 70-74,
1117 LISBOA CODEX. Tel. 360582/3

SINGAPORE – SINGAPOUR
Information Publications Pte Ltd,
Pei-Fu Industrial Building,
24 New Industrial Road N° 02-06
SINGAPORE 1953, Tel. 2831786, 2831798

SPAIN – ESPAGNE
Mundi-Prensa Libros, S.A.
Castelló 37, Apartado 1223, MADRID-28001, Tel. 275.46.55
Libreria Bosch, Ronda Universidad 11, BARCELONA 7.
Tel. 317.53.08, 317.53.58

SWEDEN – SUÈDE
AB CE Fritzes Kungl Hovbokhandel,
Box 16 356, S 103 27 STH, Regeringsgatan 12,
DS STOCKHOLM. Tel. 08/23.89.00
Subscription Agency/Abonnements:
Wennergren-Williams AB,
Box 30004, S104 25 STOCKHOLM.
Tel. 08/54.12.00

SWITZERLAND – SUISSE
OECD Publications and Information Center
4 Simrockstrasse 5300 BONN (Germany). Tel. (0228) 21.60.45
Local Agents/Agents locaux
Librairie Payot, 6 rue Grenus, 1211 GENÈVE 11. Tel. 022.31.89.50

TAIWAN – FORMOSE
Good Faith Worldwide Int'l Co., Ltd.
9th floor, No. 118, Sec. 2,
Chung Hsiao E. Road
TAIPEI. Tel. 391.7396/391.7397

THAILAND – THAILANDE
Suksit Siam Co., Ltd., 1715 Rama IV Rd,
Samyan, BANGKOK 5. Tel. 2511630

TURKEY – TURQUIE
Kültur Yayinlari Is-Türk Ltd. Sti.
Atatürk Bulvari No : 191/Kat. 21
Kavaklidere/ANKARA. Tel. 17 02 66
Dolmabahce Cad. No : 29
BESIKTAS/ISTANBUL. Tel. 60 71 88

UNITED KINGDOM – ROYAUME-UNI
H.M. Stationery Office,
P.O.B. 276, LONDON SW8 5DT.
(postal orders only)
Telephone orders: (01) 622.3316, or
49 High Holborn, LONDON WC1V 6 HB (personal callers)
Branches at: EDINBURGH, BIRMINGHAM, BRISTOL,
MANCHESTER, BELFAST.

UNITED STATES OF AMERICA – ÉTATS-UNIS
OECD Publications and Information Center, Suite 1207,
1750 Pennsylvania Ave., N.W. WASHINGTON, D.C.20006 – 4582
Tel. (202) 724.1857

VENEZUELA
Libreria del Este, Avda. F. Miranda 52, Edificio Galipan,
CARACAS 106. Tel. 32.23.01/33.26.04/31.58.38

YUGOSLAVIA – YOUGOSLAVIE
Jugoslovenska Knjiga, Knez Mihajlova 2, P.O.B. 36, BEOGRAD.
Tel. 621.992

Les commandes provenant de pays où l'OCDE n'a pas encore désigné de dépositaire peuvent être adressées à :
OCDE, Bureau des Publications, 2, rue André-Pascal, 75775 PARIS CEDEX 16.

Orders and inquiries from countries where sales agents have not yet been appointed may be sent to:
OECD, Publications Office, 2, rue André-Pascal, 75775 PARIS CEDEX 16.

68656-05-1985

OECD PUBLICATIONS, 2, rue André-Pascal, 75775 PARIS CEDEX 16 - No. 43323 1985
PRINTED IN FRANCE
(93 85 03 1) ISBN 92-64-12737-2